The Antique and Art Collector's Legal Guide

YOUR HANDBOOK TO BECOMING A SAVVY BUYER

Leonard D. DuBoff
Attorney at Law

SPHINX® PUBLISH
AN IMPRINT OF SOURCEBOOKS,
NAPERVILLE, ILLINOIS
www.SphinxLegal.com

D1509805

First Edition, 2003

Published by: **Sphinx® Publishing, An Imprint of Sourcebooks, Inc.®**

<u>Naperville Office</u>
P.O. Box 4410
Naperville, Illinois 60567-4410
630-961-3900
Fax: 630-961-2168
www.sourcebooks.com
www.SphinxLegal.com

This publication is designed to provide accurate and authoritative information in regard to the subject matter covered. It is sold with the understanding that the publisher is not engaged in rendering legal, accounting, or other professional service. If legal advice or other expert assistance is required, the services of a competent professional person should be sought.

From a Declaration of Principles Jointly Adopted by a Committee of the American Bar Association and a Committee of Publishers and Associations

This product is not a substitute for legal advice.

Disclaimer required by Texas statutes.

Library of Congress Cataloging-in-Publication Data
DuBoff, Leonard D.
    The antique and art collector's legal guide : your handbook to becoming a savvy buyer / Leonard D. DuBoff.-- 1st ed.
        p. cm.
    Includes index.
    ISBN 1-57248-349-0 (alk. paper)
    1. Law and art--United States. 2. Antiques business--Law and legislation--United States. I. Title.

KF4288.D798 2003
344.73'097--dc21
                                                    2003006274

Printed and bound in the United States of America.

BG Paperback — 10 9 8 7 6 5 4 3 2 1

Contents

Preface

It seems that people have collected items since the dawn of time. The process appears to cut across cultural lines and geographic boundaries. Even primitive societies, such as the peoples who settled North America, displayed their wealth and stature by exhibiting the spoils of war. In *The Odyssey*, Homer has an extensive discussion of the trophies collected as symbols of victory. Few collectors today are as dramatic in their methods of acquiring items for their collections as the Homeric heroes, yet, they are probably just as diligent.

This book began as the logical extension of a progression of writings for institutions and individuals involved in the world of art, antiques, and cultural property. In 1974, I was privileged to chair the first multi-national conference devoted to Art Law. Participants included leading museum professionals, international scholars, creative people, scientists, and a host of participants in the world of art, antiques and cultural property. The conference proceedings were published as a book entitled *Art Law: Domestic and International*, which, with the assistance of a National Endowment for the Arts grant, helped lay the foundation for the field of Art Law.

Through my teaching and lectures as a professor of law at Lewis and Clark Law School, I was able to develop additional material and *The Deskbook of Art Law*, now in its third edition, in two volumes, and cited by courts, the U.S. Congress, state legislatures and professionals, emerged. The Deskbook was intended to aid professionals such as judges, lawyers, legislators, museum professionals and the like with the emerging field of Art Law. Later, I wrote a book entitled *Art Law in a Nutshell* for students. More recently I wrote *The Art Business Encyclopedia* and *The Crafts Business Encyclopedia* for the creative person.

When the gallery professionals I worked with requested specific information to assist them in their activities, I wrote *The Law (In Plain English)*® *for Art and Crafts Galleries*. I also wrote *The Law (In Plain English)*® *for Crafts*, now in its fifth edition, as another book in that series.

I believed that all aspects of the field had been provided for but, to my chagrin, I learned that the collectors, perhaps the most active participants in the marketplace, had not been served. I, therefore, began work on this *Antique and Art Collector's Legal Guide*. It is intended to provide you, the collector, with a clear understanding of many of the issues that are important in your collecting activities.

The process of collecting material, digesting it, researching issues that arise, and determining which issues are most relevant to a potential reader, particularly in a field as broad as this, is extraordinary. I was, therefore, fortunate to have the help of many colleagues and friends while working on this book. It is impossible to identify all of the individuals who have contributed to this work, but there are some who deserve special mention.

I would, therefore, like to thank my colleague, Christy O. King, Esq., a principal in the firm of The DuBoff Law Group, who has spent many off-duty hours running down information which appears in the pages that follow. Her knowledge, skill and dedication are unsurpassed.

I would also like to thank Peggy Reckow for her skill in converting my scraps of paper, incomprehensible interlineations and cryptic notes into a readable manuscript. Nancy Walseth, Esq., has devoted many hours to assisting me in compiling much of the material appearing in these pages and putting that material into an understandable form.

Lynn Della, who has worked with me for years on many of the books noted above, continues to provide me with priceless aid and assistance with my writing activities. Her knowledge of the field of collecting, along with her communication skills, make her a rare find.

Gregory Roer, a Seattle, Washington CPA, has been kind enough to review the tax issues discussed in this volume. As pointed out in this book, it is important to always obtain the best, and that is what I did when I requested input from Greg. He is a brilliant accountant, and his help with the accounting material that appears in this volume is greatly appreciated.

I would also like to thank Bert Krages, Esq., the attorney/literary agent who was able to place this book with a wonderful publisher. As an author of books for publishers and writers, I feel qualified to identify Bert as a truly exceptional literary agent who does a first-rate job for his author clients.

I would also like to thank my children, Colleen Rose DuBoff, Robert Courtney DuBoff and Sabrina Ashley DuBoff, and my grandson, Brian Michael Haak, for their understanding and cooperation. There were many days when I remained closeted in my study working on this volume instead of spending time with them.

Finally, I would like to express my sincerest appreciation to Mary Ann Crawford DuBoff, my partner in law and in life. Mary Ann is also an active participant in the world of collecting. Through her buying service, Globe Galleries, she has firsthand knowledge of the needs and wants of collectors. She has provided me with more support, aid, assistance and collegiality than any person has a right to expect. Her fingerprints and golden touch are evident in virtually every part of this volume. One could not ask for a better collaborator in life's activities.

Leonard D. DuBoff
Portland, Oregon
2003

Introduction

The material that appears throughout this book is applicable to all levels of collectors, as well as to all forms of art, antiquities and other collectibles.

Whether a collector is interested in acquiring an inexpensive collectible or a museum-quality masterpiece, the same rules and precautions regarding acquisition apply. Thus, both the amateur collector and the dedicated professional should evaluate the quality of the work and determine whether it is what it is represented to be.

Once the item is acquired, precautions should be taken to be sure that it is cared for properly. The material contained in this text will aid any collector in understanding the rules, laws and practices surrounding the acquisition and sale of collectibles, crafts, art and antiquities.

This book is laid out in a logical order. It begins by considering pre-purchase issues and underscores the importance of engaging in due diligence evaluation before the acquisition. It then considers various methods of selling and acquiring items from various sources, including traditional brick-and-mortar galleries and online auctions.

Once the item has been acquired—inventorying, insuring, and conserving a collection are important and are addressed. The tax issues surrounding the purchase and sale of collectibles are outlined, and the myriad problems that can and do occur when items are entrusted to others are discussed.

In addition, the investment aspects of collecting, as well as problems that may result from the copyright and other intellectual property laws are considered. Throughout this book, the reader is provided with a clear and understandable analysis of legal and practical issues that affect collectors, collecting, and the world of collectibles.

SECTION 1

Acquisition and Protection

The first eight chapters of this book are designed to provide an understanding of the fundamentals of being a collector and the general legal issues surrounding buying and owning art, antiques, and other collectibles. This will assist a first-time buyer by giving direction to focus his or her search and will make any buyer more savvy in future purchasing endeavors.

One of the most frequently used methods of purchasing art and collectibles is by auction. The auction process can be daunting. It is filled with customs and unspoken rules that have been known to intimidate otherwise sophisticated purchasers. Even experienced auction goers can fall prey to unscrupulous auctioneers and other bidders. After reading this section, you will be able to spot questionable tactics used at auction and know what to do. You will also know how to ensure that the piece you are buying is authentic and what to do if it turns out to be a fake.

Valuable information on protecting your collection is also discussed. Specific advice is given on what steps can be taken to secure your home as well as how to properly insure against any loss.

Securing your financial investment is not only about protection, but also about conservation. Care must be taken to conserve your collectible—be it a painting, a piece of furniture, or a figurine. Knowing what not to do is just as important as knowing what to do.

The saying that an ounce of protection is worth a pound of cure is never more true than when dealing in art. Let these first eight chapters be your first source of protection.

CHAPTER 1

Getting Started

While there are many considerations to being a collector, to take on that role you must begin collecting something. You may have already decided on what you like and want without even realizing it. Take a look at your home or office decor. Where do your tastes lie? Perhaps you have always liked a particular style or media, but have yet to make that first purchase. Either way, your first step is to research.

Research

Read about the arts, crafts, antiques, or the categories of collectibles that you decided on. Your local public library will have books on history, artists, craftspeople, studios, manufacturers, and the market, as well as dictionaries defining art terms. It will also contain books on all types of collectibles. Many museums also have libraries which are open to the public. (For a list of museums throughout the world, including regional directories, see Appendix D.) Read the arts section of your local newspaper, which will probably contain a calendar of events and reviews of local and regional exhibitions.

Arts, crafts, antique and collectibles magazines, available by subscription or at the library, are also useful resources. Most public libraries have a directory of magazines that will aid you in identifying the best magazine(s) for your interest area. If you have chosen a certain medium to collect, consider subscribing to specific magazines such as *Metalsmith* or *Sculpture*. (See Appendix B for addresses and phone numbers.)

INTERNET

The Web is also a great resource for researching collectibles. You should also surf the Web for similar information and perhaps buying opportunities. *e-Bay* has one of the best sites for determining availability of all collectibles.

Museums, historical societies, libraries, auction houses, galleries, and associations have websites, which can be valuable research tools. Learning about your collectible is as easy as hooking up to the Internet. Many collectors participate in chat rooms and forums to discuss availability, price, and characteristics of their collections.

AUCTION CATALOGS

Auction catalogs are another good resource. These catalogs provide information about available items, as well as current prices. Catalogs are generally supplemented by a *post-sale sheet* listing the price at which each item sold.

TELEVISION

Television also offers learning opportunities. Public television and other stations devote programs to antiques and collectibles. For example, PBS has developed a following for its popular *Antiques Roadshow* and its companion program, *Antiques Roadshow UK*, both of which provide viewers with information about antiques and collectibles. It also provides some viewers the opportunity to have their own items evaluated when the traveling show is in their locale. There are also special programs about antiques and collectibles on cable television.

GALLERY OPENINGS

Aspiring, creative people will probably not be discussed in national publications. Local gallery shows may be the only way for you to find out about these artists and craftspeople. In many cities, galleries coordinate openings to occur on the same evening, so that collectors can go gallery-hopping. You will not only see what is out there, but can also meet the creators and other collectors. Ask each gallery if it publishes a newsletter for its patrons and, if so, add your name to the mailing list. If you are interested in the work of a particular creative person, return to the gallery carrying that person's work and request to see his or her portfolio. This will give you an idea of the range of work available.

These files often include press clippings about the person, as well. Ask for any available catalogs of the person's work and be sure to find out whether he or she works in any other media. If paintings are out of your price range, you might consider purchasing drawings or prints by the same artist.

ANTIQUE SHOPS

Visiting antique shops, malls, and secondhand stores can help you locate antiques and collectibles—often at fair prices. Frequent exposure to the vast array of available items will tend to refine your taste and make you a more discerning collector. It will also help you to establish a rapport with the staff, who may be willing to help you find specific items. In fact, many dealers will actually search for items that they feel will be of interest to their regular customers.

MUSEUMS AND HISTORICAL SOCIETIES

Most local museums and/or historical societies offer memberships that are well worth the cost. You will have access not only to the permanent collections and traveling exhibitions, but also to lectures, subscriptions, and institutional publications. Many museums and historical societies arrange tours for their members and other events that present opportunities to meet other collectors. Most museums and historical societies also sponsor special-interest affiliates such as, an *Oriental Study Society* or a *Civil War Arms Study Society*. Try to visit museums and historical societies when traveling, as well.

Purchasing

Novice collectors are probably most familiar with buying from art galleries, craft and antique shops, and specialty stores. However, there are many sources available to assist your search for that perfect piece.

IDENTIFYING REPUTABLE DEALERS

You might ask other collectors, as well as museum or historical society personnel, for the names of reputable dealers who specialize in the type of art, antiques, or collectibles you are interested in. Newspapers and specialty magazines sometimes publish lists of highly regarded dealers, so you should also do some research at your local library. Check with your local Better Business Bureau, professional associations, and the consumer protection division of your state's attorney general's office, to determine whether any complaints have been filed against a particular dealer.

Another good resource is professional organizations. Contact these organizations in order to obtain a list of its members. Such associations include the Art Dealers Association of America, the National Antique and Art Dealers Association of America, the Association of International Photography Art Dealers, the American Numismatic Association and the America Philatelic Society. (See Appendix A for addresses, phone numbers, websites and email links.)

Remember, however, that while these membership lists are a good place to start your search, membership does not guarantee a dealer's integrity, and many reputable dealers are not association members.

Once you have compiled a list of dealers to consider, you should visit each one. Ask about the dealer's return policy. Reputable dealers are willing to refund your purchase price if they sell you a fake or forgery. Some dealers will also allow you to trade in a item which, for whatever reason, you no longer wish to own. A dealer should also be willing to commit to writing any oral description he or she has given you about the work, and should be willing to allow you to consult experts before you make a purchase.

ART AND CRAFT EXPOSITIONS

Although the most obvious place to buy art is at a gallery or shop, many other possibilities exist. You should consider attending art and craft expositions. These expositions are where many galleries pick up the works that they then offer for sale. Art expositions include *Art New York*, *L.A. (Los Angeles) Expo*, *Chicago Art Expo* and *Art Asia* in Hong Kong. These expos have both wholesale and retail days, although collectors are generally allowed to view and buy only on retail days.

Many crafts expos also have retail and wholesale days, such as *ACC (American Craft Council) Fairs* and *Beckman's Gifts Shows*. Others, such as the *Buyer's Market of American Crafts*, have only wholesale days. Art and craft magazines, as well as art-event calendars (such as the *National Calendar of Indoor-Outdoor Art Fairs*) give information on dates and locations of these shows. (see Appendix B.)

Antiques can be found in antique shops, but searching garage sales, rummage sales, and the like can be more exciting. Finding a heretofore undiscovered gem is both rewarding and fun. Specialty stores which carry the collectible of your interest may be available, but you will likely pay top dollar.

There are many collectors' expos conducted throughout the country. These exhibitions are broad-based, covering every type of collectible. You should check the appropriate section of your local newspaper or online for shows in your area. Show promoters also frequently advertise on radio and television. For example, the largest antique and collectible show in the West is in Portland, Oregon each July; this show has more than 1,800 dealers offering items for sale to the general public. For other references, go to the Internet and check www.antiquesandfineart.com.

AUCTIONS

Auctions are another common place to buy art, antiques and collectibles. Large auction-houses, such as Sotheby's and Christie's (see Appendix B), offer works in every category, from Old Masters to contemporary items—furniture, books, autographs and virtually every form of collectible. Locally, check your telephone yellow pages or online for the names of auction galleries in your area. In addition, museums sometimes sell pieces from their collections through public auction.

Try to meet local auctioneers known for handling impressive estate sales. It is well worth a dedicated collector's time to ask to be kept apprised of potential opportunities. While you will not be offered a better price on items, you will be kept informed about upcoming sales and availability.

DIRECT FROM THE ARTIST

If you are interested in buying the work of a living artist or craftsperson, consider buying *directly* from that artist or craftperson. That person will be able to tell you more about the work than a dealer or auctioneer will, and you are assured of *authenticity*. An artist or craftsperson will occasionally offer you a better price on a direct sale, but most will not undercut their dealers.

A growing means of exposure to new artists and craftspeople are so-called *alternative spaces*. Alternative spaces are typically former public buildings or warehouses renovated to provide studio and display space to unknown artists and craftspeople at minimal cost. One example is the Torpedo Factory Art Center in Alexandria, Virginia. Leading alternative spaces are indexed each year in *Art in America* (see Appendix B), along with conventional commercial outlets for artworks.

Collectors may also find works of art and craft displayed for sale at banks, restaurants, hospitals and hotels. Such work is customarily labeled with the creator's name and address, along with its price.

Keep your eyes open when you travel on business or vacation. In another city, you may find a better price on a certain type of collectible or an opportunity not available in your home town.

The Internet is also becoming a wide-spread source for artists to market their works. Many artists have their own website from which purchases can be made. The Internet can also be used to identify artists outside of your normal sphere of contacts.

INTERNET

The Internet is a valuable resource. Beyond merely finding an artist, you can, through online auctions and collectors' groups, have access to virtually every category of art, antique, or other collectible. In addition, the Web is an extremely efficient vehicle for researching prices, availability and other information related to your chosen category of collectible.

By monitoring online auctions, you can conduct price comparisons. Since these auctions generally run for several days, research can be conducted in order to determine whether you wish to participate in a given auction. The pressure of a live auction is, thus, eliminated. It is not necessary to be spontaneous, since instant response is not required.

The Web is also useful when you desire to upgrade your collection, by giving you a global marketplace to acquire better quality pieces and dispose of those pieces you no longer want. Many of the sellers online are not professionals, and are merely "trading for their own account."

There are some risks associated with online transactions. Buyers cannot kick tires or bite coins in order to evaluate the merits of the item being sold. They are limited in their ability to evaluate the credibility of the seller. Sellers cannot normally evaluate the financial ability of the potential purchaser. Steps have been taken to deal with some of these obvious risks in online transactions. For example, eBay, the most popular online auction service, has established a rating program for its sellers. Additionally, online transactions have unique problems concerning the payment for the goods sold. It is wise to understand some of the payment options available, and what protections they may bring.

ESCROW

Escrow arrangements can be established as a means of protecting both buyer and seller. An *intermediary* (trusted by both parties, because it is a professional institution with some credibility) can act as an *escrow agent*, agreeing to retain the purchase price in trust until the purchaser has had an opportunity to examine the item being sold in a secured setting. Only when the purchaser agrees to accept the item will the escrow agent release the funds to the seller and permit the purchaser to obtain possession of the item.

Of course, this type of arrangement is cost-effective only for "big-ticket" items, and not every seller may agree. If the seller is reluctant to participate in this type of arrangement, it does not necessarily mean the transaction is flawed, but the buyer should always beware. It is appropriate for the buyer and the seller to share the cost.

CREDIT CARDS

Another protection for purchasers is to pay by credit card. In this type of arrangement, an aggrieved purchaser can rescind the transaction within six months if the item is not what it was represented to be. Here, too, there is a cost associated with the transaction. Sellers typically absorb this cost, but the price of the item will generally reflect it.

MEET IN PERSON

If the buyer and seller are in the same geographic region, the parties can choose to meet and complete the transaction in person. This is possible, but not common.

——◇——

There are more formal arrangements for purchasing and selling art and antiquities. Collectors should familiarize themselves with the laws, as well as the conventions, surrounding the various methods of acquisitions. In the pages that follow, many of the legal and practical considerations are discussed.

CHAPTER 2

Purchasing and Reselling Your Collectibles

Collectors should be familiar with the laws governing the sale of art, antiques, and collectibles before purchasing or reselling any such item. In additional to the legal restrictions discussed in this chapter, a diligent purchaser should avoid acquiring an item which has been stolen. (See Chapter 3 for a discussion of the laws governing misappropriated and/or stolen works.)

Galleries and Shops

Whether you intend to purchase work from or sell work to a gallery or other dealer, you need to understand the legal relationships existing between dealers and their suppliers.

CONSIGNMENT

Most often, dealers purchase so-called *fine art* on *consignment*. In fact, twenty-eight states and the District of Columbia have passed legislation establishing a *presumption of consignment* on delivery of artwork by an artist to a dealer. Although these laws do not apply to works delivered by collectors to dealers, consignment is the norm in that situation, as well.

The definition of *dealer* varies from state to state, but in general, covers anyone who holds himself or herself out as having skills as a dealer. In addition, many of the laws cover crafts, as well as traditional fine art.

Consignment is also used for other valuable collectibles such as autograph collections, coins, stamps, antique and classic cars, and the like. Consignment means the dealer will not actually buy the work; but rather, the dealer will make the item available for sale on behalf of the owner.

Remember this special relationship while negotiating the price for a consigned work. Many purchasers make the mistake of treating the dealer either as their own representative or as an independent third party when, in fact, the dealer is the seller's representative.

Consignment creates a special relationship between the dealer and the work's owner in which the dealer acts as the *owner's agent*. (In Maryland and North Carolina, however, the dealer is designated as a *bailee* of the seller rather than an agent. See Chapter 13 for more information on *bailment*.) This agency relationship means that the dealer is required to forego all personal advantage aside from being paid for his or her services.

A collector purchasing works in Connecticut, New Jersey, or Florida will be able to spot consigned works with ease, since these states require notice to the public that the work has been consigned. Notice is generally provided by attaching a sign or tag to the work or by posting notice to that effect in the exhibit space.

Generally, when you are selling a work on consignment, the dealer is your agent, and as such, must act in your best interests and under your direction. In return, you must pay the dealer a *commission* when the work sells. A dealer's commission is most commonly 50% of the selling price, but ranges from 30% to 60%.

Remember that your property will be in the dealer's possession before you are paid. An obvious risk is that the dealer could sell the work without paying you. There is also the risk that creditors of the dealer may seize the item if the dealer goes bankrupt.

Always obtain a written consignment agreement containing a description of the work, the length of consignment, the price, method of payment, and whose insurance will cover the work. Be sure you con-sign items only to reputable dealers.

In order to protect yourself from the dealer's creditors, be sure to comply with *Article 9* of the *Uniform Commercial Code* as it has been enacted in your state. The Uniform Commercial Code (UCC) is a body of commercial law which has been developed by the Uniform Commission on State Laws. Each state must consider the uniform statute and, if acceptable to the state legislature, adopt it. There are several versions of the UCC currently enacted throughout the country since many states have modified the uniform law in order to have it conform to that state's local rules, and different versions of this law were enacted at different times. It is, thus, impossible to provide the reader with an analysis of all versions of the UCC enacted throughout the country in a book such as this, but some general guidelines may be useful.

If you comply with the UCC's requirements, including filing a financing statement with the appropriate government office (usually the secretary of state or county clerk), you will likely be protected from the dealer's creditors. Contact a business lawyer the first time you consign an item, so that you can learn exactly what your state requires and the pro-cedure for complying with the UCC.

Filing a financing statement will not protect you if a dealer sells a work and does not pay you.

Some states have enacted artist-dealer consignment statutes that may be available for creative people who are covered by the law. Unfortunately, they do not protect collectors. (see Appendix C.)

OUTRIGHT PURCHASE

In an *outright purchase agreement*, the dealer buys an item from the seller, then resells it. Although this gives you the advantage of payment up front, you may be giving up some of your potential return, as there is no way to know exactly what the price the item will bring on resale.

Dealers generally pay sellers a smaller percentage of the expected ultimate sale price when purchasing a work outright than when they take it on consignment. *Outright purchase* is more common when dealers acquire craft art directly from the craftsperson (as opposed to traditional *fine art*) and when dealers buy collectibles from their owners or from estates.

Whether you are purchasing a work that was consigned to the dealer or one that the dealer owns outright, first determine whether there are any legal obligations attached to your purchase. For example, you may be subject to resale royalties or other reserved rights on behalf of a living artist (see Chapter 10).

Remember that if the work has been consigned to the dealer, the dealer's bargaining leeway may be limited by the consignment contract.

Also, what appears to be a *fixed price* may actually be negotiable. Many dealers will discount an asking price by 10% or more. These discounts may be given to other dealers, frequent customers, to those who pay cash, or on items that have proved difficult to sell.

Although some dealers require immediate payment, many will permit you to pay over time. You will typically have to sign a contract stating that *title* remains with the dealer until your last payment is made.

Artists and Craftspeople

A collector may wish to purchase a work directly from its creator. If you are able to buy directly from the creative person who is represented by a dealer, do not expect a lower price, since few are willing to undercut their dealer's prices. Some artists and craftspeople have *exclusivity contracts* requiring payment of the dealer's commission whether or not the dealer participated in the transaction. You will, however, have the advantage in a direct purchase of being able to talk with the creative person about the work and of assurance of the work's authenticity.

Commissioning a Creative Work

Occasionally, a collector will commission the creation of a specific piece. Because a work exists only in the mind of its creator until it is actually completed, it is difficult, if not impossible, for you to know what the commissioned work will look like.

If you do commission a creative work, it is important to have an attorney draw up a contract providing that you do not have to accept the work unless you are satisfied with it. In this situation, most courts will allow you to reject the work even if any other collector would be satisfied, because the contract provides that you personally must be satisfied.

What if the artist or craftsperson refuses to create the work—can you sue to require its completion? The answer is no. Although you may be entitled to monetary damages, courts will not require the artist or craftsperson to complete the work. (See Chapter 10 for more information on the artists' rights.)

Auctions

Auctions are a popular method of buying and selling art, antiques and collectibles. About half of the art sold in the U.S. is sold at auction. Because works of art, antiques and other collectibles are subject to fluctuation in market price, auctioning is especially useful for these kinds of transactions. Auctioning establishes a market value for particular types of work, indicated by what competitive bidders are willing to pay.

Another reason for the popularity of auctions is the wide variety of services offered by *auction houses*. Major auction houses often employ a complete staff of experts and have facilities available for researching, appraising, advertising, and selling any item. Catalogs advertising auction house sales are widely distributed and are often posted on the Web. Larger auction houses with galleries in several locations may transport a piece to the best place for its sale and often advertise the sale on its website. Some houses even offer lectures or courses and sponsor worldwide tours of collections. Most auction houses also have *pre-sale online catalogs* and *post-sale prices.*

An auction house also may provide or facilitate financing. At one point, Sotheby's financial policy even allowed buyers to use property they planned to purchase as collateral on loans from the auction house.

For instance, the 1987 sale of Vincent van Gogh's Irises *was made possible by a $27 million loan from Sotheby's, with the painting itself used as collateral.*

This policy of extending loans to buyers against art being auctioned was modified following industry criticism that such arrangements inflated prices in the art market. Sotheby's still allows purchasers to use items as collateral, provided they have been wholly owned for 90 days or more.

Many *auctioneers* act as *independent contractors* and their services can be procured for either a fixed price or a percentage of the amount of auction proceeds. They will conduct the auction at the seller's residence, place of business, or anywhere else the seller may reasonably request. The services of auctioneers are commonly sought for *estate sales* and *business liquidations.*

TYPES OF AUCTIONS
Although the form of bidding varies from place to place, there are four particularly common techniques.

English or Ascending-bid Method
In the *English* or ascending-bid method, the auctioneer first solicits a bid. If there is no response, the auctioneer suggests an opening bid, which is lowered until adopted. Once a bid is made, the auctioneer either allows *free bidding* or guides the bidding by calling out the *next acceptable bid.* The purchaser is the person who makes the last and highest bid.

Dutch or Descending-bid Method

In the *Dutch* or descending-bid method, the auctioneer announces an opening figure and then lowers the price until a bidder accepts. Because the first, rather than the last bidder obtains the item, you must accurately evaluate the competition.

Japanese or Simultaneous-bid Method

In the *Japanese* or simultaneous-bid system, an auction is customarily a closed, invitation-only affair run by dealers for dealers. All bids are entered at the same time, using either hand signals or sealed bids. The auctioneer then determines who offered the highest bid during the short time period permitted for bid entry. The seller may either accept the highest bid or withdraw the piece.

Online Auctions

Online auctions are similar to the English auction style, but employ technology as the auctioneer. Bidders who have signed up with an online auction house post their bid. The bidding remains open for a prescribed period of time. The last highest bid that exceeds any *reserve price* will be accepted by the seller. The purchaser must then complete the transaction in an off-line arrangement.

The rules for participating in an auction, whether online or in a brick-and-mortar setting, vary from auction house to auction house, and, thus, it is essential for you to familiarize yourself with the rules before participating in a particular auction. For example, some auction houses provide that consigned items must sell or the *consignor* must nevertheless pay a specified fee. Many auction houses impose a *buyer's premium* on sales; that is, an amount, usually a percentage, over and above the successful bid price.

Today, most brick-and-mortar auction houses have websites. They may use the sites for purposes of advertising upcoming auctions, posting catalogs and/or announcing post-sale prices. Some may permit remote or *absentee bidding* though the site, or even conduct online auctions.

AUCTION BASICS

Auction houses generally do not own the works of art they sell. Typically, the works are on consignment. In other words, the auctioneer is the agent of the seller until a sale is made. Once the auctioneer accepts a buyer's bid, the auctioneer must consider the interests of the buyer as well as the seller when making and signing the contract for sale.

If you are consigning an item to an auction house, the commission you must pay may be negotiable, especially if the piece is particularly valuable. Many auction houses also charge for catalog photos, insurance, and transportation costs. These fees may also be negotiable. You will typically receive payment from auction sales between one week and one month after the sale.

Remember that the sale is likely to occur weeks (or even months) after you arrange for the consignment.

Once items to be sold are assembled, auctioneers and their staff carefully examine and evaluate the pieces. Experts may be consulted to determine the identity and authenticity of an unknown work. If there is any disagreement within the auction house as to the auction appeal of the consigned property, the house has a duty to disclose this disagreement to the consignor.

Furthermore, once the auction house accepts the property, the auction house should disclose to the seller the risk that the property may be *branded as burned*. This means the property may lose value if it fails to sell.

Once all items are accepted, a catalog may be prepared and made available to interested persons. Many collectors throughout the world subscribe to auction catalogs. This allows them to monitor price trends and developments, as well as to determine whether to bid on any specific item. While there is a charge for catalog subscriptions, participation in auctions themselves are generally free. Tickets sometimes are required, but usually are free. It has also become quite common for auction houses to post online catalogs and post-sale prices. Auction catalogs themselves have value, and those describing famous sales have become collectible. For example, the catalog for the Jacqueline Kennedy Onassis sale has become particularly sought-after.

Online Auctions

Online auctions have become quite popular. Virtually every form of collectible can be obtained at an online auction. Bidders may be required to register with the auction house and also may be required to establish some creditworthiness such as by use of a credit or debit card. Similarly, sellers of items to be auctioned must be registered with the online auction house and may establish a rapport with the gallery through their business practices. Some online auctioneers, such as eBay, actually have a rating system for sellers.

One of the advantages of shopping online is that no *buyer's premium* is imposed by most of the houses, nor is there state sales tax added, as of this date, and the variety and availability of collectibles is vast and ever-changing. Online auction buyers have been successful in finding undiscovered treasures at bargain basement prices. The difficulty in buying online is that the item cannot be examined for quality or authenticity, and there have been many instances where buyers were misled about the quality or other characteristics of an item, and some cases where items were not delivered. Online auction escrows have been developed to overcome some of these problems.

One of the few distinctions between online auctions and brick-and-mortar auctions is the fact that some online auctions allow the purchaser to pay a specified or *buy now price*. This is almost never done in a brick-and-mortar auction for art,

You should determine whether the online auction house you are dealing with has a policy for returns, non-delivery, misrepresentations and the like. If it does not, then caveat emptor (buyer beware) should be your motto.

antiquities and other collectibles, since all of the items available there are intended to be sold through traditional auction methods.

Occasionally, brick-and-mortar auctions will permit pre-auction *buy now* arrangements. The *buy now* price sometimes listed on an online auction can be offered at any time in order to acquire the item and complete the sale for that price. Frequently, this *buy now* price is comparable to the reserve price set by the seller.

RESERVE

As an auction consignor, you will probably want to set a *reserve price*, a minimum price below which the item may not be sold. The auction house may guide you in determining a proper reserve. The auction house will, in theory, bid on the work until the reserve has been met, but drops out of the competition at that point. This is because, until the reserve price is matched, the auction house will not sell the item to any bidder. If the bidding does not reach the reserve, the auction house makes the last bid, and the property is *bid-in* or *passed*, meaning the item was not sold.

For this protection, you will be required to pay a commission based either on the reserve amount or the last independent bid, depending upon the policy of the auction house and/or your consignment agreement. The percentage charged is generally less than the percentage to be paid if the work had sold. The *bid-in* item may then be returned to the seller, sold privately, or offered again at a later date.

Prospective bidders should be informed that the auction is *with reserve* before the bidding begins. In some states, however, all auctions are presumed to be with reserve unless otherwise announced. New York City regulations require auction houses to identify those items in their auction catalogs that have a reserve, although they are not required to state the reserve amount. As a guide to buyers,

Bidders assume the risk that the item may be withdrawn before being sold.

auction catalogs present low and high estimates of sale-price predictions. Reserves at the major auction houses are generally lower than the low estimates.

Generally, online auctions follow the same practice and disclose whether an item is subject to a reserve, and, as the auction proceeds, whether or not the reserve has been met.

Withdrawal of Goods

If a sale is without reserve, the auctioneer can withdraw the item only if no bid is made within a reasonable time. Otherwise, the sale must be made to the highest bidder. The vast majority of auctions, however, are conducted with reserve. In this situation, as noted above, the seller has the right to withdraw the goods from sale even after being placed on the block if the reserve price is not met.

Goods may also be withdrawn where the seller reserves the right to refuse any bid made. The seller may exercise this right even after the auctioneer has accepted a bid.

Online auctions may follow different procedures with regard to withdrawal. You should, therefore, determine the site's policy with respect to this issue.

PRICE GUARANTEES

Some auction houses will guarantee a certain sale price. If the sale price exceeds the guaranteed amount, the auction house charges, in addition to its usual commission, a percentage of the amount by which the sale price exceeds the guaranteed price. If bidding does not reach the guaranteed price, the auction house pays the consignor the difference between the sale price and the *guaranteed price.*

VIEWING OF GOODS

All auctions have previews of the goods offered for sale. Online auctions and brick-and-mortar auctions houses with websites may post pictures of the items being offered, and do provide written descriptions.

While some expensive items or pieces of fine art may be displayed for days ahead of time, pre-auction viewing for most auctions takes place either the day preceding or in the two or three hours before the auction.

Because auctioned merchandise is usually sold *as is*, it is important that prospective bidders inspect those items they are considering buying. In the case of online auctions, there is no preview; rather, the picture and description are posted when the time for bidding begins. Customarily, items are auctioned according to their order in the catalog in live auctions.

Since the auction norm, as–is purchase, is also the norm online, care should be taken to determine what the return policy is for purchased items.

BIDDING

At live auctions, bids may be either disclosed or undisclosed. In *disclosed bidding*, potential buyers openly compete in an attempt to outbid one another. The oral bid is used most frequently, although use of raised cards or paddles is also common.

In *undisclosed bidding*, secret bids are submitted, often by a sealed writing, a hand signal or a whisper. The auctioneer then compares bids without disclosing them. Undisclosed bids have some disadvantages, most notably the fact that auctions involving them are very time-consuming to conduct. Sealed bidding provides each bidder only one bid.

An auctioneer may simultaneously use both disclosed and undisclosed bidding. For example, hand signals may be used by a certain bidder at an otherwise oral auction in order to help keep that bidder's identity secret. For those who cannot attend the auction in person, they may submit written, or absentee, bids in advance of the auction. The auctioneer is then authorized to bid up to the designated amount on behalf of that bidder. Auction houses also may accommodate those unable to attend by using telephone hookups, or in some cases, online connections, to allow participation in the bidding.

Because of concealed bidding, the name of the successful bidder may not be known when the gavel falls. In addition, there is usually no announcement if an item does not sell. In either case, the auctioneer may or may not say "sold," and may or may not identify the buyer. Auction-goers may find it nearly impossible to discover the results of the auction until the post-auction sales sheet, if any, is released by the auction house.

With online auctions, bids are always posted and the bidding is left open for a specified period of time. While the identity of the bidder may not be known, the price the item fetches will usually be posted when the auction closes. Online auctions may post the results of an auction after the bidding has closed, but such a posting will likely be for only a limited period of time.

WITHDRAWING BIDS

The highest bidder may withdraw his or her bid until the auctioneer accepts it. If a bid is withdrawn, all other bids for that item are considered to have lapsed. In other words, the second highest bidder must give his or her consent in order for the auctioneer to accept that bid.

AFTER THE AUCTION

If you are the successful bidder, you may be asked to sign a *bid confirmation form*. An auction house usually requires a successful bidder to pay either a set amount or a percentage of the purchase price as a gesture of good faith to bind the contract. If your credit has not been pre-approved, you probably will be required to pay the full purchase price before taking possession of the item.

In the event the buyer is unable to pay the agreed price, the deposit is generally forfeited, although your bid confirmation form may provide otherwise. Auction houses have the discretion to cancel a sale if the buyer does not pay. The auction house is not required to pursue a defaulting buyer for payment, although it may choose to do so.

Many auction houses, including Sotheby's and Christie's, charge a *buyer's premium*, generally 8% to 10% and some go as high as 12% to 15% over and above the purchase price. You will also be required to pay state and local sales tax.

When bidding, remember that the actual amount you pay will likely be higher than your bid.

TACTICS

Bidders and auctioneers alike will employ various tactics to affect the sales price. Some of these tactics are perfectly legitimate; for instance, inexpensive items may be introduced early and sold rapidly to establish a fast-paced tempo of sales. You should be aware, however, of unscrupulous practices, and how to avoid them.

Auctioneers

One fraudulent technique is for the auctioneer to recognize *phantom bids*. *Bidding off the chandelier*, as it is known, occurs often enough that experienced buyers sit as far back in the auction room as possible in order to see the competition.

The auctioneer may also place a *confederate* in the audience who bids solely to encourage high bids from genuine bidders. In this situation, an excited bidder is actually bidding against him- or herself. Such puffing or shilling is illegal and will entitle the buyer to rescind the transaction or to take the goods at the price of the last good faith bid. The buyer loses the right to these remedies, however, if he or she accepts the contract with knowledge of the puffing.

One tactic used to inflate prices for unknown items is to mix them with recognized treasures. Where an auctioneer intends to deceive a bidder by this practice, fraud will likely have been committed. Nevertheless, the vast majority of these situations go undetected. In fact, even when they are detected, proving that the auctioneer intended to deceive the bidder is very difficult.

Another technique that can affect the ultimate and future sales price occurs when the prices published after the auction are inaccurate. There have been instances where reports of sale prices at auction were actually the results of private post-auction sales of items that did not reach the reserve price in bidding. Although the private sale price likely differs from the *hammer price*, it may be recorded in the post-sale catalog as the price reached in bidding at auction. Both Christie's and Sotheby's have acknowledged that they may record private transactions occurring after auction as actual auction sales.

Bidders

Not every auction-goer is looking for a bargain. Collectors or dealers may bid without intending to buy in order to ensure that a certain work maintains or increases its value. More often, however, collectors and dealers try to keep prices low.

For instance, a bidder might make disparaging remarks to mislead other prospective buyers regarding the worth or authenticity of the object. Bidders with limited resources may strategically avoid bidding on small items, hoping the competition will purchase them before the higher-priced items are placed on the block. Where the presence and interest of a known dealer or collector might spark excessive bidding, that person may have an agent bid for him or her, or may participate by telephone.

Another common practice having an affect on price is *joint buying*. If this arrangement is intended to alleviate the inconvenience of attending the auction or to reduce transaction costs, then it is legal. If, however, buyers combine intending to depress prices, the arrangement is probably illegal. The essential feature of a *ring of buyers* is the secret agreement among the participants not to compete against each other, thus controlling prices so that they remain low.

Rings are illegal by statute in Great Britain. Although there is no special legislation in the United States directed against ring operations, many believe that antitrust laws adequately cover this situation.

As a seller, you should try to protect yourself against rings by setting a reserve price. Another precaution is to consign work to well-publicized auctions by major houses, where it is less likely that a ring will be able to control prices. This is because major houses have experience in identifying rings and dealing with them. If the auction is well publicized, then the crowd is likely to be larger, and experienced auctioneers will be able to determine whether the volume of bidding on an item is normal or artificially reduced through ring activity.

Perhaps the best advice that can be given a newcomer to the auction world is to be alert and exercise extreme caution in this unique market.

General Restrictions

There are legal restrictions on the purchase and sale of certain items. A few examples:

The Native American Graves Protection and Repatriation Act (NAGPRA) restricts the trade of artifacts excavated from government or tribal lands after November 16, 1990. It also bans the purchase or sale of human remains or of "associated funerary objects"—that is, objects which were buried with human remains, regardless of when they were excavated, unless permission is granted by the descendants or the appropriate tribe;

Sale of items containing materials from endangered plant and animal species are generally prohibited. (See Chapter 12 for more details.) A number of import and export laws restrict trade in some art and antiquities, as well. (see Chapter 12.) For more information about these and other restrictions, see the Federal Bureau of Investigation web site, www.fbi.gov.

CHAPTER 3

Due Diligence on Purchase and/or Sale

Before purchasing a work of art or any collectible, it is essential for the purchaser to determine that the work is authentic and that it is legally transferable. In addition to the legal restrictions discussed in Chapter 2, the law may provide some protection for those whose items have been stolen. It is clear that a collector whose works are stolen may recover the misappropriated items from the thief, yet, in most instances, the items will have been resold by the thief to others. It is well-settled that no one can acquire a *good title* from a thief, yet this rule is not as protective as one might think.

Stolen Goods

In a case involving works of art and valuable antiquities acquired from representatives of the former Soviet government, it was held that, since the items had been nationalized by the legitimate government of the country, the original owner did not have a valid claim of theft and could not recover the items taken from her family, nor could she recover damages. This case should be distinguished from cases involving art looted by the Nazis during World War II from occupied countries. Since the Nazis were not the legitimate government representatives of the occupied territory, it was held that their expropriations were unlawful and that individuals who were able establish title to looted works can recover them.

There is a split of authority throughout the United States regarding the ability of original owners of stolen goods to reclaim those items when located in the hands of *innocent repurchasers*. The New York rule is that the original owner must first demand the return of the misappropriated item, and that demand refused, before a *bona fide repurchaser* will be deemed a wrongdoer. In the majority of jurisdictions, however, the rule is that the original owner may reclaim a stolen item. This applies even if the purchaser acquired it in good faith without any reason to believe that the item was stolen. The aggrieved repurchaser may have recourse against the person or entity from whom the work was purchased or the thief, but not against the legitimate owner. It is for this reason that extreme diligence is necessary before acquiring art, antiquities or other collectibles.

You should always deal with reputable sellers who will be available to assist you if the title to a particular item is later challenged.

In addition, purchasers should check registries of stolen works when available. Unfortunately, these registries frequently are limited to noted art and antiquities, and do not include most other types of collectibles. (see Appendix D.)

Despite your precautions, you may acquire a work that is later discovered to have been stolen, forged, an infringement of another's copyright, or a fake. If this occurs, you should first request a refund from the seller, since a reputable dealer should be willing to offer you an exchange or cash refund. If, however, the seller is unwilling to reimburse you for the cost of the item, you may be able to recover your loss by bringing a lawsuit under the Uniform Commercial Code (UCC). (The UCC is a law governing commercial transactions, including warranties on sale, and has been enacted by every state except Louisiana, though it has a similar body of commercial law.)

Warranties

A *warranty* is, in essence, a guarantee that the item you purchased will be of a certain quality or have certain attributes, such as a painting having been painted by a certain artist or an antique being of a certain age. This guarantee may be oral or in writing (it will, of course, be easier for you to prove if in writing), or even implied by law.

A successful lawsuit brought under the UCC will allow you to recover the difference between the value of the item you actually received and the value as if it had been as the seller warranted. This means that you are entitled to the benefit of your bargain.

> *For instance, say you paid $10,000 for a certain work, knowing that if everything the seller warranted was true, it was actually worth $20,000. Later you discover that the work is a forgery, worth only $500. You might think you could recover only $9,500, but under the UCC, you could recover $19,500 ($20,000, the value of an authentic work minus $500, the current value).*

Unfortunately, the UCC does not provide aggrieved purchasers with the ability to recover the attorney fees that they must incur in litigating a warranty dispute. The American rule is that each party is responsible for that party's own attorney fees. This rule can be modified by the parties if they agree in writing that, if there is any dispute, the prevailing party will be entitled to recover, in addition to any damages awarded, the reasonable attorney fees and costs incurred in litigating the dispute.

Not every statement made by a seller will be construed as a warranty, and not every item you purchase will be covered by a warranty. Many sellers try to disclaim or eliminate all or some warranties. Some guidelines for deter-

Disclaimers of warranties are effective if they meet UCC requirements, so pay careful attention to statements made by the seller, as well as to any written material you are given.

Remember that many of these same laws apply when you are selling items from your collection. Be careful, or you may be held liable for breach of warranty.

mining whether a valid warranty or disclaimer exists are discussed below, but you should contact a business lawyer before purchasing a particularly expensive item or if you discover that you have purchased a stolen, forged or infringing work.

EXPRESS WARRANTIES

Any factual statement or promise that describes a item will create an *express warranty*. It is not necessary that the seller use the word warrant or guarantee, or that the representations be written into the contract. Express warranties can arise from oral statements or from representations in advertisements or catalogs. For instance, an oral statement that a piece of glass art was created by a certain artist or a catalog representation that a sculpture is the second in a limited edition of ten may create an express warranty. You will have to prove, however, that you knew about and relied upon the representations.

You must also distinguish between a factual statement or promise, which creates a warranty, and mere opinion, or sales talk, which does not. Unfortunately, no clear standard has yet been determined by the courts. One factor considered is the relative knowledge of the buyer and seller. For instance, is the seller an expert and the buyer only a novice? In that situation, a court is more likely to find that a statement created an express warranty. If the seller tells you "it is only my opinion that this piece of stemware is Steuben," that may not create a warranty, but if a knowledgeable seller tells you "this piece of stemware is Steuben," then it is likely that a legally enforceable warranty has been given.

Express warranties of authenticity are especially troublesome, particularly in the case of older items, since it is difficult, if not impossible, to know for certain that a work is authentic. Even experts are fooled by high-quality fakes and forgeries. Many, therefore, argue that express warranties of authenticity generally are not created by such representations.

Because of the difficulty in applying the UCC's warranty provisions to art fraud, some states have legislation dealing specifically with art warranties. New York, Michigan and Florida have enacted laws providing that an art merchant who sells a work to a non-merchant buyer creates an express warranty of authenticity if, in a written description of the work, he or she identifies it with a certain artist. Other forms of collectibles have not yet obtained similar statutory protection.

Even if you cannot successfully argue the existence of a legally enforceable warranty, you may nevertheless be able to *rescind the purchase.* You would then return the work and the seller would return your purchase price. Rescission is available where you can show that both you and the seller were honestly mistaken as to an essential attribute of the item, such as its authenticity.

Express warranties generally may not be made and then later disclaimed, though they can be clarified.

IMPLIED WARRANTIES

The UCC also provides for four types of implied warranty: warranties of non-infringement, title, merchantability, and fitness for a particular purpose. These warranties are created by law even if the seller makes no such representations.

The phrase as is *or* with all faults *will exclude all implied warranties when stated in connection with used items, although this applies only where the buyer has had a full opportunity to inspect the item.*

Warranty Against Infringement

When an item is sold, the seller implicitly warrants that the work is not infringing any rights protected by patent, trademark or copyright. (See Chapter 9 for more information on copyright infringement.) This means that, if you buy a work of art from a dealer and later discover that it is an infringing copy of another artist's work, you may be entitled to recover damages and you will have a defense to any infringement action brought against you. Similarly, if you buy a device which is later established to be an infringement of another's valid patent, you may return it to the seller and receive a refund of the purchase price. You may also recover any amounts you were forced to spend other than for attorney fees as a consequence of the breach of implied warranty.

This warranty is implied only to sales by merchants (including manufacturers, galleries, dealers, auction houses and retailers). So, if you buy a work from a non-merchant collector, you should request from the seller an express warranty against infringement.

This warranty is important, because a court could order your infringing piece destroyed. In addition, by reselling an infringing work, you may be guilty of infringement, as well. Since you could be liable for far more than the value of the item (your remedy under the UCC), you should obtain an express warranty against infringement, if possible. This warranty should provide that the seller agrees to reimburse you for any expenses you may incur because of the infringing work, including any attorney fees. Your lawyer can draft such a warranty for you. An implied warranty against infringement can be disclaimed by a seller by explicit language.

Warranty of Title

When you buy an item, you assume the seller had the right to sell it to you. Unfortunately, this is not always the case. To protect purchasers, the law implies a *warranty of title*. This warranty is breached when the seller either does not have good title or does not have the right to convey the item. This means that, when you are required to return a stolen work to its original owner or when you discover that the purchased item was not wholly owned by the seller, you will have an action against the seller for reimbursement.

For example, the Norton Simon Foundation purchased a 10th century bronze sculpture of Siva (a Hindu deity) for $900,000 from art dealer Ben Heller. The country of India, the work's rightful owner, sued for the return of the sculpture, known as the Nataraja. A settlement was negotiated, in which the Norton Simon Foundation agreed to return the Nataraja to India after being permitted to display it for ten years. The Foundation was able to recover from the art dealer for his breach of the implied warranty of title.

A seller can disclaim this implied warranty by specific language or the warranty may be negated by circumstances that give the buyer reason to know that the seller either does not have title or is only selling the title to the portion he or she owns.

Warranty of Merchantability

The *warranty of merchantability* applies only when you purchase a work from a merchant. This warranty may apply to protect purchasers of forgeries. An item is considered merchantable if:

- ✦ it passes without objection in the trade under the description given in the contract;
- ✦ it is at least fit for the ordinary purposes for which such items are used; and,
- ✦ it at least conforms to the promises of fact made on any container, package or label.

If you acquire a forgery that has been considered authentic for a long time, the warranty may not appear applicable, since the work has arguably passed "without objection in the trade." The work would still likely not be considered fit for the "ordinary

A signature on a forged work or a descriptive plate on the base or frame of a fake may give rise to a claim for breach of warranty, since merchantability requires that the work conform to any representations made on its label.

purposes for which such goods are used," however, since an ordinary purpose probably includes the aesthetic pleasure of an authentic work, and certainly includes investment potential.

A disclaimer of the implied warranty of merchantability is enforceable only if it specifically mentions the word *merchantability*. This disclaimer may be oral, but if it is written, it must be conspicuous. Say, for instance, that you purchased from a merchant a painting with a descriptive plate stating that it was painted by Rembrandt. This normally creates a *warranty of merchantability* protecting you in case the painting is a forgery, but you may lose that protection if the dealer tells you, or the receipt states, that the warranty of merchantability is disclaimed, that merchantability is not guaranteed, or the like. An express warranty, however, may still exist, unless the written disclaimer is effective in negating that warranty, as well.

Warranty of Fitness for a Particular Purpose

A fourth implied warranty is *warranty of fitness for a particular purpose*. To establish a breach of this warranty, you must prove that:

→ the seller knew of your particular purpose;
→ the seller knew that you were relying on the seller's skill and judgment; and,
→ you actually relied on the seller's skill and judgment.

A *particular purpose* is different from the *ordinary purpose* covered by the warranty of merchantability and, in the case of art and collectibles, probably does not include investment potential or aesthetic enjoyment. On the other hand, if your particular purpose was to obtain a certain piece or complete a specific collection, you may be protected by this implied warranty.

It is best for a collector to obtain a document listing the material attributes of the work purchased, such as its age, authorship, medium, and the like. As discussed in Chapter 4, problems with incorrectly stated edition size of multiples have become so widespread that many states have enacted laws that require the use of some kind of certificate disclosing certain relevant facts about the multiple. (see Appendix C.) Artists and craftspeople who are sensitive to the concerns of collectors and who wish to make the art they create more marketable customarily provide certificates of authenticity accompanying their work. Many antique dealers follow a similar practice.

These certificates customarily contain a description of the item and may also contain maintenance and conservation instructions, as well as an explanation of what the creator was thinking about when the work was created, the date the work was completed, and where it was completed.

These documents add to the provenance of the work and help a collector establish a file that should accompany the item when and if sold or resold.

This warranty may be disclaimed, but the disclaimer must be in writing, and must be conspicuous. The language fitness for a particular purpose is not required.

CHAPTER 4

Authenticating the Work

The emergence of art, antiques, and collectibles as investment vehicles has stimulated an increase in forgery—an estimated 15% of all art, antique and collectible transactions involve forgeries or fakes. The amount of money to be realized from a successful forgery can be substantial and no doubt serves as the major incentive for unscrupulous individuals. Since the value of collectible items is determined partially by aesthetic appeal and partially by the work's *provenance*, it is of paramount importance to a purchaser that the piece's authenticity be ascertainable with a high degree of certainty. Clever and talented forgers often have made this determination extremely difficult, even for experts.

Forgeries

There are three general categories of forgeries:

+ fabrications deliberately created to be sold as the product of another, with an intent to deceive, including the forging of a creator's name, the work's documentation, or the entire work;
+ replicas, reproductions and copies, created without an intent to deceive, which are ultimately sold as originals due to misattribution or error, including works executed *from the school* of a famous person which are later sold as an original;
+ altered items, including embellishments, fragmentation of oversized pieces, completion of unfinished works, and excessive restorations.

Hans Van Meegeren had a successful career as a forger of Vermeers, a famous 17th Century Dutch painter, and was discovered only when he himself disclosed the frauds. Charged by the Dutch government for aiding the enemy during World War II by selling Dutch treasures to the Nazis, Van Meegeren was defended by stating that he cheated the Germans by selling them fake Vermeers. The art world, shaken by the news, refused to believe him until he created a masterpiece in his jail cell, proving his claims to be true. Sophisticated scientific tests confirmed additional forgeries. The Van Meegeren *Vermeers* may have some value for their historical significance and notoriety, but certainly not the worth of recognized Dutch Masters.

Another notorious forger, David Stein, adopted the styles of many noted artists, forged their signatures and sold the works he created as authentic. Stein's skill was extraordinary and he continued to work even while confined in prison, although those works bore the caption, *Forgeries by Stein*. Over half of Stein's *Forgeries* sold on the first night they were offered for sale.

Other examples include situations where, for example, bronze recasts which are originally labeled as such are altered to remove the *restrike* identification marks and sold as originals. Similarly, Cola-Cola collectible serving trays from the early 1900s are being reproduced, with notations indicating that the reproduction is a copy. Unscrupulous individuals have been known to remove or obscure the *copy* marking.

PROTECTIONS

Federal and state anti-fraud statutes provide some sanctions against forgery, but the penalties are slight compared to the potential profits which may be gained by creating and successfully disseminating fakes. In addition, these statutes all require proof of a fraudulent or criminal intent. This element is easily established in the case of the forger, but is more difficult to prove when applied to the intermediate seller, who may not even suspect the spurious origin of the object.

Several precautions can be taken to reduce the likelihood of acquiring a counterfeit piece. Gain a familiarity with the style, period and creative peculiarities and, if possible, compare the desired work with known forgeries, as well as authentic pieces. Several museums have arranged to show collections of fakes as a service to the public in order to provide an opportunity to become acquainted with the most frequent stylistic errors of forgers.

Preventative measures aimed at making forgeries more difficult to pass off are by far the best protection for collectors.

You also should question the seller regarding the name of the creator or manufacturer, a description of the piece, the date of its execution, the existence of historical records indicating the chain of ownership (provenance), and the genuineness of the signature or identifying marks. Collectibles may have legally been manufactured by several companies, but some may be more valuable than others.

Records of a work's provenance are useful, although not foolproof, tools in authentication. Some works will be accompanied by letters, bills of sale, labels or other documents. These records may indicate which dealers, auction houses or museums have sold or exhibited the work. Because these documents themselves could be forgeries, you should contact each dealer, auction house and museum, if possible, in order to verify the information. It is a well-known adage that all fakes have impressive provenances.

In some cases, dealers and auction houses will refuse to tell you the work's provenance. This may be because it is unknown or because it is undesirable. Another possibility is that the work was recently purchased for far less than the alleged value.

You should be wary of a situation where a dealer refuses to verify the accuracy of his or her representations about a work, or where the dealer claims to have no knowledge of the work. Although this does not necessarily mean that the work is a fake, it does mean that there is some irregularity—*caveat emptor* (buyer beware). You should take whatever precautions you deem necessary in light of the price of the work.

When buying online from, for example, eBay or one of the other reputable auction sites, you should be sure that the seller will allow return for full credit after you have had a reasonable opportunity to examine the work. Never pay for an item purchased online before examining it, other than by credit card. If the seller will not allow an escrow arrangement for big-ticket items, be cautious. When using credit cards, if the work turns out to be a fake or otherwise not as represented, you have six months within which to rescind the transaction and the credit card company will *charge back* the amount of the purchase.

If the creator is living or still in business, you may request a *certificate of authenticity* and or similar authentication for "big-ticket" items, which should accompany the piece whenever it is resold or transferred. The certificate of authenticity should include:

> ✦ the name of the creator;
> ✦ the title or description of the work;
> ✦ the date and place of completion;
> ✦ a description of the subject matter;
> ✦ materials or media used;
> ✦ a statement of the rights reserved by the creator, if any; and,
> ✦ a signature warranting that the work is genuine (if possible).

If the sale is made by a dealer and the creator's signature is unobtainable, the seller may give a *warranty of authenticity*.

EXPERT EVALUATION
In addition to relying on personal knowledge, consult an expert. This type of expertise falls into two general categories: stylistic and scientific. *Stylistic authentication* results from a subjective evaluation of the work by a historian based on knowledge, intuition and experience.

Scientific authentication, on the other hand, results from an objective evaluation of the work based on the results of assorted scientific tests performed on the work.

The differences between these methods occasionally result in insoluble conflicts, particularly when the scientific data contradicts an expert's stylistic opinion. These two approaches are not, however, mutually exclusive. One method can complement the other and lead to an even more accurate determination.

STYLISTIC

A historian relies on a mental data bank to relate an object under study to other cultures, periods and creators. Of course, any data bank's reliability depends on the quality and amount of information it contains. The comparison method, where the most minute details of a work are examined in conjunction with the details of authenticated works by what is believed to be the same creator, is the most useful and popular method.

The threat of time-consuming and costly litigation, however, makes many honest experts reluctant to render opinions at all. Museum personnel, potentially an excellent source of information for a prospective purchaser, are prohibited by their employers from giving opinions to outsiders. Many private experts refuse to contradict even blatantly incorrect reports of other experts for fear that litigation will result or that their own reputation may be compromised. It is therefore, difficult, if not impossible, to have a newly discovered piece conclusively identified and authenticated. It is more common for experts to say only that, based on the accumulated data, a work is more likely to have been created in a particular period by a particular creator than any other.

A collector who employs an expert to authenticate a piece and later discovers that the work is not what it was represented to be may seek redress from the expert. A collector also may sue because of disparaging remarks made by an expert.

In a 1929 case that rocked the art world, the art expert Duveen settled out of court for $60,000 for statements he made about the collector's painting. Duveen, a stylistic expert who had never actually viewed the painting, claimed that it had not been painted by Leonardo da Vinci and that the original was actually in the Louvre. The owner, Hahn, alleged that her property rights had been violated when Duveen falsely and maliciously stated to a newspaper reporter that the Hahn picture was not genuine. Hahn added that these statements induced a museum to call off negotiations then in progress regarding its purchase of the work.

Duveen, on the other hand, contended that his First Amendment right of free speech would be destroyed if statements of opinion could not be made in good faith regarding a picture that was before the public for sale and that had been the subject of newspaper articles in America and France.

Duveen presented a *fair comment defense*. Fair comment or criticism on a matter of public interest is not actionable so long as the comment is not motivated by actual malice.

The essential elements of the "fair comment" defense are:

→ that the statement is an opinion;
→ that it relates not to an individual, but to his or her acts;
→ that it is fair, namely, that the reader can see the factual basis for the comment and draw his or her own conclusion; and,
→ that the statement relates to a matter of public interest or to anything submitted to the public, such as books, art exhibits and musical performances.

If, however, the defendant's statements were made with actual malice, that is, with knowledge of their falsity or in reckless disregard of the truth, the fair comment defense is not available. Further, professional critics should not be allowed to rely on the fair comment defense when their statements are based on conduct that does not meet professional standards. Since Duveen was a stylistic expert who had never even viewed the piece in question, his conduct was quite unprofessional, making his fair comment defense inappropriate.

An expert less than thorough in the methods used to determine a work's authenticity or in making an appraisal may face a charge of professional negligence by a disappointed buyer. On the other hand, a thoroughly professional evaluation resulting in an honest opinion should not subject the expert to liability, even though the opinion may be contrary to the belief and expectations of the party who hired the expert.

In a 1982 case, a first-time fine art purchaser who, by his own admission, knew nothing about art, acquired at an auction for $17,000 what he thought was a painting by Sir Joshua Reynolds. He hoped for a high appraisal of the work, which he would then donate to a museum and thereby receive a high charitable tax deduction. His plan was frustrated when the auction house's expert appraised the painting for only $30,000 (instead of the $200,000 hoped for) and indicated that, in her opinion, the painting was by Tilly Kettle, not Reynolds.

The buyer then sued the appraiser for negligence and slander of title, alleging that the appraisal had caused him financial loss. The court disagreed. The court felt that the appraiser had performed her job as adequately as could be expected under the circumstances. She had conducted in-depth research, referred to the standard texts and references, and spoken with the recognized authority on Reynolds' works. No more could be expected of her, so her conduct was not negligent.

SCIENTIFIC

Scientists may rely on a host of established tests in order to evaluate authenticity. Depending on the work to be authenticated, any number of different tests can be used.

Radiocarbon

One of the best-known techniques used for authentication is *radiocarbon dating*, which measures a type of radiation known as carbon-14. It is, however, applicable only to date organic material. This process can, therefore, be used to date wood, paper, leather, hair, shells and bones, including ivory, which are between a few hundred and 40-50,000 years old. Some forgeries cannot be detected by this method, however, because forgers sometimes create their forgeries using materials from the appropriate time period.

Thermoluminescent Analysis

Thermoluminescent (TL) analysis is used to date ceramic ware, such as fired clay or porcelain, by heating a sample and measuring the emitted TL. This will give the time elapsed since the last firing of the clay. TL analysis covers age periods ranging from about 300 years to that of the oldest pottery known.

Comparative Analysis

The principle of the *comparative analysis* technique of dating is to develop characteristic composition patterns. This test may yield strong proof that a work is a forgery where, for example, it is found that certain compounds did not come into existence until after the alleged date of the work.

Reconstruction of Manufacturing

A similar idea is behind *reconstruction of manufacturing* technology. Works may be shown to be forgeries if they were manufactured using a process not yet developed at the supposed time of the manufacture.

Microscopic

Microscopic techniques may be used to discover the type of material, as well as various indications of age, such as the formation of dendrites, which are quartz crystal growths.

X-Rays

X-rays provide remarkable insight into the structure of paintings, often revealing underlying brush strokes and, in some cases, even fingerprints of the artist. *X-ray diffraction*, used to discover material composition, has been used in the detection of faked *patina* on bronzes. *Autoradiography* reveals structural details of paintings and their supports. This analysis permits the identification of a number of the pigments used in painting, and gives information on the manner in which they were originally applied by the artist.

Other methods

Some methods occasionally used for dating art works, but more often used by archaeologists and geologists, include chemical analysis (useful mainly for dating fossilized bones), obsidian hydration analysis (for dating obsidian), fission track analysis (for dating objects from 70,000 to approximately one million years old), and the potassium-argon dating test (for dating igneous and sedimentary rocks).

These and other methods allow scientists to date the materials used in the works, as well as to examine the external and internal structure of the works. While these tests may be feasible when a major work of art is involved, their costs will generally outweigh their utility in the case of minor acquisitions.

Of course, the costs of evaluating the authenticity is a function of its worth and, thus, its potential value. It would not be cost-effective to conduct expensive scientific tests for the pur-

The collector must evaluate the cost of analysis versus the risk involved.

pose of authenticating, for example, a Star Wars action figure, though it may be reasonable if the purchaser is acquiring a truckload of them. One organization that offers authentication for owners, their representatives and authorized potential buyers is the International Foundation for Art Research (IFAR). (see Appendix D.)

Multiples Legislation

In many states, dealers of editioned prints are required by law to disclose certain information to help protect collectors and other buyers from misrepresentations. California, Georgia, New York, and Michigan have enacted *multiples* laws which cover sculpture, as well. (see Appendix C.)

Generally these laws require the seller to provide a buyer with a certificate, invoice, or receipt that contains certain specific information regarding the work. The information required customarily includes:

→ the name of the artist;

→ the year the art was created;

→ whether the edition is limited;

→ the present status of the plate or mold;

→ whether the work has more than one edition and, if so, the edition of the work, as well as the size of the edition;

→ whether the edition is posthumous; and,

→ identification of the workshop or foundry where the edition was printed or cast.

Many of the statutes also require information about the medium or process used, such as whether the print is an etching, engraving, woodcut, or lithograph, or whether the bronze is hot or cold cast, or whether the dealer does not know. Some states require disclosure of the method of affixing the artist's name to the multiple (whether signed, stamped, engraved or molded). Unless disclosed, the number of multiples described as being in a limited edition shall constitute an express warranty that no additional numbered multiples of the same image have been produced.

If the edition is limited, further disclosures are required, including the maximum number of releases (both signed and unsigned), the number of proofs allowed, and the total edition size.

The majority of statutes provide that describing the edition as an edition of *reproductions* eliminates the need to furnish further informational details.

All the statutes provide that a person violating the disclosure requirements shall be liable for the amount the purchaser paid, plus interest from the date of purchase. In some states, a wronged purchaser can recover three times that amount.

Even if your state does not have a multiples law, you should try to get in writing as much of the above information as possible. Without this information, you cannot determine whether you are being charged a fair price for the work and, unless the representations are made in writing, it will be difficult to prove that you have been misled.

You should be aware that, in some states, these laws also apply to collectors who sell multiples. You should, therefore, check local laws or contact an attorney before selling any multiples from your collection.

Certification Marks

Another method of minimizing the problem of fakes and forgeries is the establishment of *certification marks*. These marks may be used to identify authentic works and to impose penalties for the mark's improper use. The Indian Arts and Crafts Board, which is a branch of the U.S. Department of the Interior, has done this for Native American arts and crafts by adopting a certification mark which can be used only by Native Americans to identify their works. Penalties are imposed for violation of the statute. Alaska has adopted a similar form of legislation for its native peoples.

Conclusion

While there are laws that can be used to aid you in recovering the amount by which you have been cheated if you acquire a fake or forged work, some elements of the case may be difficult to prove and recovery may involve high litigation costs. It is, therefore, more prudent to take as many precautions as possible when acquiring a work of art, antique or other collectible. Prudence should be the byword for collectors. For more information, you should check online, since there are numerous collectors clubs which are generally eager to share their knowledge and experience. In addition, there are a host of publications covering virtually every form or type of collectible. Public libraries, as well as museum or historical society libraries, have a fair collection of specialized books and most contain auction catalogues, which can be very helpful in identifying prices, dates of sale and the like.

Be as knowledgeable as you can about the artist or manufacturer, medium and age of the piece, and insist on having all representations about the work put in writing.

In today's world of computer technology and sophisticated methods of replication, there is a great risk of having a new generation of fakes and forgeries. Even diamonds can be manufactured in a lab, and science marches on. It is, therefore, even more important for a collector to be prudent, verify provenance, and carefully evaluate the legitimacy of virtually every item before it is acquired.

CHAPTER 5

Inventory and Insurance

Once you have made that decision to buy your first big piece, or whether your smaller collection is growing in size, you want to take steps to protect it from loss or theft. Knowing what records to keep and understanding the basics of insurance principals is a must for any collector.

Inventory

You should keep an up-to-date inventory of the items in your collection, complete with the prices you paid, and the last appraised value or believed market value. You should keep the bill of sale, with any certificate of authenticity, along with other documents establishing provenance, if any. If you purchased at a live auction, keep the catalog description and your receipt. If you purchased on an online auction, print out the online auction information. Your records should also include appraisal documents, photographs, historical letters describing the work, and the like. They may be kept in a safe deposit box or other secure place. You may also wish to have a video made of your collection. This will aid in identifying any stolen pieces and assist restorers if a work is damaged.

Records concerning inventory, market value, and authenticity should not be kept with the collection.

Insurance

Because even a modest collection can become quite valuable, you will probably want to insure all or part of your collection. Even in rural areas, you may become the victim of burglary, or suffer from fire, flood or earthquake.

WHAT AND WHEN TO INSURE

The most elementary way to determine whether the value is sufficiently high to necessitate insurance is to rely on the pain factor: if it would hurt to lose it, insure it.

Three factors should be weighed to determine whether or not to obtain insurance. First, you must set a value on that which is to be insured.

Second, you must estimate the chances that a given calamity will occur. An insurance broker can tell you what risks are prevalent in your neighborhood. You should supplement this information with your personal knowledge. For example, you may know that your home or office is virtually fireproof, or that only a massive flood would cause any real damage. If the odds are truly slim, but some risk is still present, the premium will be correspondingly smaller in most cases.

Consider that art theft is now the second largest international trafficking crime (after drugs), and that only 5% to 10% of stolen artworks are ever recovered.

The third factor is the cost of the insurance. Bear in mind that this cost may be tax-deductible. (See Chapter 11 for more details.) For instance, if you are allowed the deduction and you pay tax at a rate of 36%, the government is essentially paying for 36% of your premium.

WHERE TO BUY INSURANCE

Insurance is available through three primary sources: independent agents, brokers, and directly from the insurance carriers through their agents. Since independent agents and brokers can write insurance for a number of insurance companies, they are less likely to be biased and will probably be in a position to provide you with the best advice. (For the name of at least one company specializing in insurance for collectibles, see Appendix D.)

THE BASICS OF INSURANCE LAW

You should be aware that public policy will not permit you to insure something unless you have an insurable interest. You have an insurable interest where you personally would suffer a loss if the risk covered by the policy came to pass. This restriction is intended to minimize the temptation to cause the calamity against which you are insured.

All insurance is based on a contract between the insurer and the insured whereby the insurer assumes a specified risk for a fee, called a *premium*. The insurance contract, or policy, must contain at least the following:

- a description of whatever is being insured (the subject matter);
- the nature of the risks insured against;
- the maximum possible recovery;
- the duration of the insurance; and,
- the due date and amount of the premiums.

When the amount of recovery has been predetermined in the insurance contract, it is called a *valued policy*. If there is a total loss, the insurance company may not contest the amount unless fraud was involved. An *unvalued insurance policy* covers the full value of property up to a specified policy limit.

The insurance industry is regulated by state laws. These laws require that premiums be set using a certain method and usually specify the training necessary for agents and brokers, the amount of commission payable to them, and the kinds of investments the insurance company may make with the premiums.

THE CONTRACT

Even the documents that a company uses to make insurance contracts are regulated. Sometimes the state requires a standard form from which the company may not deviate, especially for casualty insurance. A growing number of states require that all forms must be in plain English. Nevertheless, insurance policies remain difficult for the average person to interpret.

One frequent result is that the signed contract may differ in some respect from what the agent may have led you to expect. If you can prove that an agent actually lied, the agent will be personally liable to you for the amount of promised coverage, in the event of a claim.

Most often the agent will not lie, but will accidentally neglect to inform you of some detail. For instance, if you want insurance for transporting collectibles, the agent may sell you a policy that covers transport only in public carriers—although you intended to transport the collection yourself, in your own vehicle or a rented truck. In most states, the courts hold that it is your duty to read the policy before signing it. If you neglected to read the clause that limits coverage to a public carrier, you likely would be out of luck.

In other states, this doctrine has been considered too harsh. These states will allow you to challenge specific provisions in the signed contract to the extent they do not conform to reasonable expectations resulting from promises that the agent made. In the preceding example, it might be considered reasonable to expect that you would be insured when transporting collectibles. If the agent did not specifically bring to your attention this limitation you may have a good chance of not having that limitation applied against you in the event of a loss.

You should always review the contract with the agent. If it is unintelligible, ask the agent to list on a separate sheet all the important aspects before signing, and then keep that sheet with the contract. Certainly, if you buy insurance and do not receive the actual policy until later (or never receive it), you will likely be able to rely exclusively on the agent's representations.

Keep in mind that representations and statements being made flow in both directions. If the information you give the agent contains omissions or incorrect statements, coverage may be lost. The courts have various criteria for determining whether or not an omission or incorrect statement renders a policy void. In all cases, however, the omission or incorrect statement must be intentional or obviously reckless, and must be material to the contract. If stating the fact correctly would have significantly affected the conditions or premiums that the company would demand, then the fact is material.

REFORMING THE CONTRACT

After the insurance contract has been signed, its terms can be reformed (revised) only to comply with the original agreement from which the written contract may somehow have deviated.

> For example, consider the case of a woman who inherited a pearl necklace and was told by an appraiser that the pearls were genuine and worth $60,000. The woman insured the genuine pearls for $60,000, paying a premium of $2,450. When the pearls were ruined, the woman tried to collect the $60,000. It was discovered that the pearls were cultured and worth only $61.50. The woman could not collect $60,000 because no genuine pearls were lost or damaged; she could not collect even $61.50, because the policy did not cover cultured pearls. Reformation of the contract could not be granted, since neither party ever intended to insure cultured pearls. The court also found that because the pearls' true value would never have come to light if they had been lost instead of destroyed, the insurance company had indeed assumed the risk of paying out $60,000 and thus was entitled to keep the premium.

OVERINSURING AND UNDERINSURING

The example on the previous page does not mean that if you accidentally overvalue goods, you will lose coverage. Had the pearls been genuine, but worth only $20,000, the woman would have recovered $20,000. Overinsurance does not entitle you to a recovery beyond the actual value of the goods.

Because you can, at best, only break even with insurance, you might think it would be profitable to underinsure your goods, pay lower premiums, and lose only if the damage exceeds the policy maximum. This, however, may be considered fraud, and void your entire policy.

A coinsurance clause generally provides that the insured may recover 100% of any loss up to the face value of the policy, provided the property is insured for a stated percentage (usually 80%) of its full value.

> For example, if a collection worth $100,000 were insured for $80,000 and suffered a $79,000 loss from a covered casualty, the insured would recover the full amount of the loss: $79,000. If the collection were insured for only $50,000, a formula would be used to determine the amount of recovery: divide the amount of insurance coverage by the total value of the property; multiply the resulting fraction by the loss. In this example, $50,000 (insurance) divided by $100,000 (value of collection), times $79,000 (loss), equals $39,500 (recovery).

You can see why it is important to carry insurance on at least the minimum percentage required.

Many insurance contracts allow some undervaluation where it is immaterial and unintentional. This provision is designed to protect the insured from inflation and appreciation, which causes property to increase in replacement value before the policy's renewal date. Considering the inflation rate and the fluctuation in the value of collectibles, it is wise to examine your coverage each year. Most insurers also provide protection for subsequently acquired works, provided that the insured reports the acquisition within a specified time (often ninety days) and pays the added premium, if any, retroactive to the time of acquisition. This is particularly important with valuable collectibles.

TYPES OF POLICIES

The typical insurance policy will include various exclusions and exemptions. For example, most homeowner policies cover personal property but exclude business property. If a collector keeps items at home for personal enjoyment, are those pieces personal or business property? The answer depends on whether the collector is also a dealer. If so, the entire collection may be considered business property.

In order to avoid a potentially tragic loss because of a technicality, you may *schedule* the works. You should submit a list and description of all pieces to be insured with an appraisal of their value. The insurance company assumes the risk of loss of all the works placed on the schedule. Insurance on scheduled property is slightly more expensive than that on unscheduled property.

Those with collections valued at more than 50% of their total personal property coverage should consider purchasing a *rider* to their homeowner's insurance policy. Riders are typically available for such high-value items as jewelry, furs, fine art, and other collectibles. The premium for a rider will typically be less expensive than the increase in the premium for a higher face value in the homeowner's insurance.

Those with collections valued at more than $1 million should work with an insurance company with special expertise in art, antiques and other collectibles. Since you are unlikely to lose the entire collection, you should consider a blanket coverage policy that pays based on current market value at the time of the loss. A blanket policy insures your collection for substantially less than the aggregate value of the works, with coverage applying to losses involving any portion of the collection up to the amount insured.

SPECIFIC PROVISIONS

Another consideration is whether you frequently lend works from your collection to museums and the like. If so, your policy should be *wall-to-wall* or *nail-to-nail*, which means that the policy will insure the works while away from the insured premises. Those who lend infrequently may depend on short-term wall-to-wall policies, or coverage by the borrower. In that event, the collector should request certification that the work is covered by the borrower's insurance company. (See Chapter 13 for more information on lending works to museums.)

Exclusions from coverage should be carefully examined. Riders commonly exclude damage resulting from repair, restoration, or retouching. Another typical exclusion is breakage of fragile articles, such as glass or marble. Coverage for breakage is normally available for an additional premium.

Another provision collectors should be aware of allows the insured to obtain coverage for a pair or set of objects. This clause entitles the insured to recover the full value of the pair or set when a loss occurs to one or more pieces, provided the insured surrenders the remaining pieces.

In addition, policies often include clauses requiring the insured to surrender items on which a total loss is assessed and full-insured value is paid. Because of these clauses, when stolen works are recovered, the insured may not get them back from the insurance company. You should negotiate a right of first refusal, so that if the work is recovered you have the option of buying it back from the carrier at the value as of the date of loss, not the date of recovery. If, however, the contract has no clause requiring surrender, you may be able to keep both the insurance money and the work.

Some collectors choose to purchase *ransom insurance*. Such policies reimburse collectors for ransom payments made to thieves in exchange for the return of their works. Because a stolen item rarely brings in more than 10-20% of its value on resale, many well-known pieces are stolen for the purpose of ransom. This type of insurance is very popular in museum insurance and increasing in popularity for important private collections. It is probably not cost-effective to maintain ransom insurance for inexpensive collectibles.

APPRAISALS

Insurance companies frequently require an appraisal of a work when a policy is issued. You should be aware that companies often require that such appraisals be made by individuals possessing special expertise with respect to the object in question and its market value. You should, therefore, determine whether your chosen appraiser is satisfactory to the insurance company before contracting to have the evaluation performed.

You should update your appraisals at least every three years, and more often if the market is volatile.

Appraisals should include:

→ the date of appraisal;
→ title of the work;
→ the creator or manufacturer;
→ the date of the work;
→ whether the work is signed;
→ a description of the work's subject matter;
→ whether the work is framed, on a base, cased, etc.;
→ the work's size, medium, and condition; and,
→ value (See Chapter 11 for additional requirements for appraisals for tax purposes.)

You should obtain two signed copies of the appraisal—one for you and one for your insurance company.

Reputable appraisers charge either a flat fee or an hourly rate. Some appraisers charge a percentage (generally, 1%-10%) of the appraised value. You should avoid these, as this gives the appraiser an economic incentive to intentionally overvalue the work. To find a reputable appraiser, consult museum officials and art dealers for suggestions or contact the Appraisers Association of America or the American Society of Appraisers for a list of their members. Telephone yellow page listings typically identify professional affiliations. You can also find appraisers online. If you are seeking an appraisal for charitable deduction purposes, contact the Art Dealers Association of America (ADAA). (See Appendix A for addresses, phone numbers, and websites.)

Be sure to let the appraiser know that the appraisal is for insurance purposes. If you anticipate needing the appraisal for tax purposes, as well, ask for both appraisals. The difference is that the insurance appraisal is customarily for *replacement cost*, while the tax appraisal is for *fair-market value*. These amounts may or may not be the same.

REDUCING THE RISK AND THE PREMIUM COST

As explained above, the premiums charged by an insurance company are regulated by state law. Nonetheless, it still pays to shop around. Insurance companies can compete by offering different packages of insurance and by hiring competent agents to assist you in your choice. Increasing your deductible is one common way to reduce premiums.

Another way to reduce your premiums is to reduce the risk of loss. Providing your insurer with a list of precautions you have taken against fire and theft may help to convince it that you are a good risk and, thus, entitled to a reduction in premiums.

Fire prevention devices include ionization and smoke detectors, as well as sprinkler systems and hand-held fire extinguishers (these, however, may cause water or chemical damage to works). Those with particularly valuable collections should consider the more expensive halon extinguishers and sprinkler systems, which will not injure collectibles.

To prevent thefts, install strong, pick-resistant locks on windows and doors, bright lights around the home exterior, and an alarm system.

Alarms which signal the presence of an intruder both by local alarm (loud noises or flashing lights within the home) and silent alarm (a signal sent to a commercial alarm-monitoring company or police department) are recommended.

Perimeter protection devices, which protect points of access to the premises, are generally sufficient. Those with particularly valuable collections, however, may choose to install interior alarms, as well. These include step mats which set off an alarm when stepped on, audio detectors, motion detectors, photoelectric systems that set off an alarm when the intruder interrupts an invisible infrared light or laser beam, passive infrared devices that are sensitive to body heat, and various sensors that are activated when the object is moved. Guard dogs may also be used to deter thieves.

Loss Occurrence

Loss or damage should be reported promptly to your insurance company. If valuable works are involved, you should ask for an adjuster who is experienced in art, antique and collectibles claims.

Report thefts to the police immediately. If appropriate, notify the online registries of stolen works. (See Appendix D, in particular, the FBI site, that discusses the steps to be taken when there is an art theft.) You also should consider notifying one or more of the clearinghouses for information about stolen art and antiques, such as the International Foundation for Art Research (IFAR), based in New York. (See Appendix A for the address and phone number.)

In a leading case, the right of the noted artist Georgia O'Keeffe to recover three paintings missing from her collection was questioned when the works were later discovered in the hands of a bona fide repurchaser. O'Keeffe had not reported the alleged theft to the police or stolen art registries when she first discovered that the works were missing.

Preventing theft is by far a better method of protecting your investment. The next chapter discusses some measures you can take to avoid having to make an insurance claim on account of theft.

CHAPTER 6

A Guide to Protecting Your Home and Collection from Theft

One of the most devastating experiences is having one's home burglarized. The feeling of vulnerability, exposure, and utter helplessness is accompanied by the realization that you have experienced a loss. Even if the house and its contents are insured, there is no coverage for your loss of time and psychological trauma. In addition, it is quite common to have a significant deductible on most insurance policies; this means that the portion of a loss equal to the deductible will be your financial responsibility.

It is, therefore, important for you to determine effective methods for decreasing your exposure to a burglary and learning the most effective methods of dealing with a burglary if it occurs. There is virtually nothing that can be done to prevent a burglary from occurring, but steps can be taken to minimize the risk.

Savvy collectors avoid being personally identified with their collections and insist upon anonymity. It is also prudent to avoid having your address published in telephone or other directories, if possible.

Anonymity

Collectors who tout their collections in newspapers or periodicals invite attention and inform potential burglars of the fact that their collections may be available. All a clever thief needs to do is ascertain the scope of the collection and use a telephone directory, either in print or online, to locate the address of the collection. The same problem occurs when collections are displayed in museums or other high-profile locations.

Alarm Systems

In addition to avoiding visibility, you should attempt to secure your house and other properties for which you are responsible. There is a plethora of alarm systems available. Some can be installed by anyone with a modicum of mechanical talent, and others require that the work be performed by a skilled professional. The triggering devices for alarm systems include everything from pressure pads to motion or heat sensors. It is not necessary to arm every door, window and vent in order to secure a building. Strategic planning and evaluation of likely entry points are important when designing an effective alarm system. In addition, alarms can be monitored by monitoring companies, such as Brinks Home Security and ADT Home Security Services, the police, or a network of neighbors.

If the system is to be monitored, it should be determined whether it is possible for a sophisticated burglar to interfere with the monitoring line and, if so, what alternatives are available. Certainly, an onsite alarm will help, but sophisticated alarm systems may have some form of bypass for situations where the principal line is interfered with. In addition, there are devices available today for communicating both alarms and video imaging over the Web as a means of establishing a secure monitoring system, though these may also be subject to interception.

Regardless of the type of alarm system installed, it is essential to make its existence notorious to potential thieves. Posting signs and labels on doors identifying the building as being protected by a monitored alarm will deter many would-be burglars since they are likely more interested in successfully completing the burglary rather than engaging in a challenging experience. Most burglars are amateurs after a quick profit rather than professionals who feel that there is some thrill in overcoming exceptional odds.

Unfortunately, this is not always the case, and it has recently been disclosed that many skilled burglars were trained by the U.S. government for special operations in military and paramilitary organizations. These individuals are likely to be far more effective than their amateur counterparts. You should also ensure that the alarm control box is not accessible to would-be burglars. It is quite simple for a thief to disarm the alarm at the control box with a piece of wire and some alligator clips.

Exterior Considerations

Another step that should be taken to secure a building is to remove all items from the exterior of the building that could be used to assist a burglar. These exterior items would include ladders, stepstools, and the like. Where possible, foliage should be cut back so that windows, doors, and other means of entering a building are visible from the street. In addition, thorny bushes planted near the building may deter climbing. It is a good idea to have a building's exterior well lit, and motion-sensitive lights are often effective deterrents. These lights should be mounted high enough so that thieves will not be able to disable them.

Doors and windows should have good locking devices. Use deadbolts on doors. The deadbolt should have at least a one inch throw. A double-cylinder deadbolt requiring a key on both sides provides the most security but is prohibited in some jurisdictions due to possible difficulties in exiting the location in case of a fire. Make sure that the doors are solid. Glass paneled doors and glass side panels flanking doors should be replaced with a shatter-resistant polycarbonate material.

Simple window locks should be replaced with more secure devices or even bolted shut. The tracks of sliding glass doors should be secured using a wood or metal bar in the track. Patio doors can be secured with pins or locks holding the moving and fixed portion together. Double-hung windows should be secured with an eyebolt fastened through the sashes where they meet. If you have a garage door opener, check to see whether your electronic door opener has rolling-access-code technology so that the remote code is automatically changed after every use.

When on vacation, do your best to make your house seem occupied. Stop mail and other deliveries, have the lawn mowed or snow cleared from the walks, and leave a car in the driveway. Be careful who you tell that you are going out of town.

Establishing a *Neighborhood Watch* can also be a good deterrent. You should try to discourage a burglar from considering your building to be an easy mark, and anything you can do to slow a burglar down if access is accomplished will be beneficial. In addition to deterrents, you should take steps to identify your property if it is stolen.

Identifying Your Property

Where possible, you should mark the items in your collection so that they can be identified as yours if misappropriated. Be careful to mark the work in such a way as to not mar its value, though permanent marking is important. In addition, other methods of identifying your valuables should be used.

Laser markings for precious and colored stones, fingerprinting the craqueture on paintings and other modern, more scientific techniques have been developed for purposes of identifying many collectibles. You can check with the curatorial staff of your local museum in order to learn what options are available for the items in your collection and where the techniques of identification, if desired, can be performed.

It is a good idea to videotape your house and its contents, focusing on the items in your collection. If you display works from your collection in your office or business location, it should be videotaped as well. Using video equipment with a soundtrack is a good idea so that you can narrate the tape, explaining where you are in the building and identifying particular items. You should cover virtually every nook and cranny of your home or commercial building and its contents. The tape should be stored in a location other than on the premises of your home or business. A safety deposit box is useful for this purpose. Similarly, the results of identifying tests should also be maintained in a secured location.

A comprehensive inventory of your collection should be maintained. You should continuously update this inventory so that it is complete and accurate at all times. If your collection is insured, the carrier will likely want to have a copy of this inventory available in the event of a loss. Some insurance companies insist upon having the inventory when the policy is first issued. Others either request or require an insured to retain the inventory in a secured location. As noted above, a safety deposit box may be the ideal place to store a video of your collection and a catalog of it as well.

Victim of Burglary

If you are a victim of a burglary, then it is essential for you to immediately notify the police and use your best efforts to alert other appropriate parties of the tragedy as well. There are many organizations identified on the World Wide Web that list collectibles that have been stolen and any rewards that might be available to persons assisting with recovery. You should also immediately, of course, contact your insurance broker or agent and follow that person's instructions with respect to the proper method of filing a claim if your collection is insured.

Cooperate with the authorities. Try not to disturb a burglary site until after the police have reviewed it and performed whatever investigative procedures they desire. Do not attempt to be a Sherlock Holmes since you may very well hamper a proper investigation and, as a result, be in violation of the insurance policy's requirement that you cooperate in the event of a loss.

The feeling of vulnerability and helplessness which often results from being burglarized is quite common. Time is often necessary to heal that wound, and taking steps to prevent it from reoccurring may accelerate your recovery. Unfortunately, this is a form of closing the barn doors after the horse has escaped and, while better than nothing, is not the preferred technique. Taking precautions before the fact is preferable. Anything that you can do to make yourself less visible as a burglary target will be beneficial. In addition, securing your property to the best of your ability is a wise move.

Unfortunately, collectors enjoy displaying their collections and sharing them with others. This will likely attract attention and, in some cases, the wrong kind of attention. It is, therefore, important to implement a security plan and be diligent if a burglary does occur.

CHAPTER 7

Investments

Throughout the centuries, the wealthy have collected works of art, antiques, and other collectibles, not only for their own enjoyment, but with the underlying knowledge that these works can be exchanged or upgraded as the buyer's wealth increases. Although the concept of purchasing purely for investment originally met with horror, it is safe to say that investing in art, antiques, and collectibles has achieved respectability. Some investment advisors encourage their clients to purchase art, antiques or other collectibles as a hedge against inflation and as a complement to a traditional investment portfolio. In addition, art, antiques and other collectibles may provide intangible dividends, such as the aesthetic enjoyment of the item or an opportunity for personal contact with an artist or craftsperson and with others knowledgeable about collecting.

Collectors

In the art market, the international center for art and antiques is recognized as being in London and, until recently, trading has been led by the Americans, Europeans, and Japanese. Due to the downturn in the Japanese art market in 1990, the Japanese have been far less active in the international art and antiques market. Investors from China and Hong Kong are expected to dominate the market in the 21st century. Corporations, banks, museums, individual collectors and funds comprise the bulk of the purchasing community, and each group influences the market in accordance with its tastes and purchasing patterns.

Only a few private collectors have the ability to compete directly with museums and corporations for outstanding works, yet a middle ground of buyers is rapidly emerging: those buyers whose incomes are far above those of the novice investor and below those of the dynastic collector. People in this category account for a large percentage of the volume of sales at both auctions and galleries.

A substantial income is not necessarily a prerequisite for the would-be collector, as collectibles are available in every price range. For example, a small, authentic 19th century oil painting can be bought at retail for between $400 and $500. Action figures may be acquired for under $5, and other collectibles, such as paperweights, can be found for as low as $1. Individuals with modest financial means can acquire sizable collections by patronizing local artists, craftspeople, consignment shops, resale shops, garage sales, flea markets, and the like. The Internet is another source of every category of collectible.

Investment Potential

As an investment vehicle, collectibles appear to perform well in inflationary times. In the long run, collectibles follow general trends in traditional investment markets but, in the short run, the collectibles market generally rises when there is a sharp decline in the stock market. This appears to be the result of a belief among some that art, antiques, and other collectibles are more valuable than money or stocks. The devaluation of currency in the United States and Europe in the early 1970s, for example, resulted in panic buying in the art and antiques market and substantial increases in the value of many antiques and other works of art. Other collectibles may tend to fluctuate in value based on other factors.

For example, the popularity of items manufactured in the 1960s has increased with the graying of the baby boom generation. As these individuals' discretionary income rises, the price of memorabilia from their youth increases.

Scarcity also affects price. Fancy scent bottles have become popular and appreciate in value because of their delicacy. Victorian garments in good condition, plentiful in the 1960s and '70s, are now difficult to find and have become quite expensive.

The rewards of investment in collectibles can be substantial. *Pick's World Current Report* analyzed price trends in 1975 and concluded that the best hedge against inflation that year was French Impressionist paintings. They rose an astonishing 230%, while the Dow Jones averaged a mere 38% increase. In periods of deflation, on the other hand, investors seek a return in money rather than in appreciation. As a result, many investment advisors counsel their clients to put no more than 10% of their assets, exclusive of real estate, into tangible investments (including art, antiques and other collectibles). Consider the 1990-91 crash of the art market, in which sales by Sotheby's and Christie's fell more than 50%.

The Internet has significantly affected the collectibles market. Online auctions have expanded the market and provided both dealers and collectors with a useful tool. As a result of this dimension, other markets, such as antique shows, live auctions and flea markets, have experienced a decline in attendance. In order to respond to the new dynamic, live exhibitions have been forced to increase quality and provide potential purchasers with items not otherwise available on the Web. The collectibles market is in flux.

The Web has also created new business opportunities for those involved in the collectibles markets. Web-based businesses, for such purposes of escrowing transactions or facilitating transactions between buyers and periodic sellers, have flourished.

Some investment advisors believe that art, antiques and collectibles are overrated as an investment. These advisors argue that collectibles indices far overstate investors' returns, since items that fail to sell are sometimes not included. Also, indices do not account for security, insurance, and maintenance costs—none of which are required for traditional investments. They also fail to account for the much higher transaction costs entailed in selling art, antiques and other collectibles—dealers may take commissions of up to 60% of the selling price. And, while most stocks and bonds earn an investor dividends or interest payments, the primary financial return on collectibles is at their sale (other investment activities may include rental of the works and licensing of reproduction rights).

Others believe the collectibles market is primarily an area of stable, but modest, returns. All agree that investing in art, antiques and collectibles is not for those hoping for large short-term returns. For example, most advisers say you should expect to hold on to a work of fine art for ten to fifteen years.

Knowing what to buy and sell, how much to acquire and sell, and when and where to purchase and sell are the keys to any successful investment. While many collectibles appreciate, it has been suggested that 98% of the works sold in a given year will decline in value. Collectors should, thus, learn all they can about the market in which they are trading.

You should know that the collectibles market is largely unregulated.

Stocks and bonds are regulated by statute and policed by administrative agencies, but there is no comprehensive body of statutes specifically designed to prohibit manipulative or deceptive practices in the collectibles market. The question arises, therefore, whether laws designed to regulate the trading of securities can be applied to art, antiques and other collectibles. Unfortunately, the answer remains uncertain. Currently, the Securities and Exchange Commission (SEC) is not working to regulate this market, although the Federal Trade Commission (FTC) is quite active.

The FTC has brought suit to stop unfair and deceptive trade practices in the selling of artworks—specifically, prints and animation cells. In one series of cases, the publisher and gallery misrepresented that work had been created, produced and/or signed by famous artists, including Dali, Picasso and Miro. The FTC was able to secure full or partial refunds for defrauded customers.

Investment Considerations and Sources of Information

Because the collectibles market is largely unregulated and because it has many unique characteristics that may be traps for the unwary, collectors should carefully evaluate their investments.

Art, antiques, and other collectibles are also not a particularly liquid investment. It may be difficult to sell collectibles for fair market value on short notice, and a year or more may be needed for the work to sustain a sufficient increase in value so that a

Investing in collectibles is a highly speculative undertaking— at best, it is a gamble. Like any investment, the higher the risk, the higher the potential return.

profit may be realized. Dealers and auction houses take commissions from between 10% and 60% of the selling price, so the piece must appreciate substantially before you can realize a return on your initial investment if selling through these professionals. Additionally, you do not have the advantage of simply picking up the telephone and being confident of a comparatively rapid sale, as with listed stocks. You must find a customer or dealer willing either to make an outright purchase or to accept the work on consignment.

Auction houses may provide a faster transaction, but it is still not an immediate sale. Depending on the work you are selling and on the auction house, the period between submission of the work and the sale of the work may range from a few days to a few months.

Selling collectibles at auction often brings a lower price than selling to or through a dealer. The market may be very limited and, in some situations, may even be non-existent. Even an online auction,

When buying collectibles for investment, keep in mind the three main factors that determine price: quality (including condition and authenticity), rarity, and demand. If an item meets the first two criteria, then demand—and with it, price—may grow.

which provides a seller with global exposure, may not solicit any real interest.

Investment advisors consistently recommend against purchasing most works in the middle range; that is, works that are neither the best nor the least expensive in any given genre of collectible. Most money in the collectibles market is made either by capitalizing on established trends or by taking big risks. Conservative investors buy only top-quality items. Speculators may take a chance on less traditional items. These investments carry the greatest risk, but offer the greatest investment potential.

Some categories do better than others. While most experts agree that collectors should simply buy what they like, it is important that you learn as much as possible about the particular type of item prior to acquiring it. A potential investor can benefit from attending auctions, exhibitions and shows, as well as lectures and classes. A great deal of information can be gathered from newspapers articles and other publications, and by surfing the Web.

A collector interested in buying the works of particular artists may write the Museum of Modern Art or the Metropolitan Museum, both located in New York City, for the names of reputable galleries displaying the works of those artists. (See Appendix A for addresses and phone numbers.) Crafts artists can be located through the American Craft Council, also based in New York (see Appendix A), and collectors of other types of items can surf the Web for information. Catalogs published by galleries and auction houses offer an excellent source of information regarding prices and availability, as do online auction sites.

Many investors use consultants to assist them in purchasing. The Museum of Modern Art in New York provides an Art Advisory Service to corporations, hoping to educate business people so they will buy daring art. Similarly, many local museums have comparable services. Most consultants are freelance advisors. Because they are not connected to any particular artist, craftsperson or sales event, as are galleries and auction houses, they are likely to give you a more complete and unbiased view of what to buy. Also, they may obtain discounts when buying from galleries.

The roles and fees of consultants vary. Their services include counseling, collection evaluations, procurement, and installation. Prices may be hourly, based on a fixed rate, or by commission. Ask for a recommendation from other collectors, or look in the telephone book yellow pages or online. Be sure to check out the background of any consultant. For instance, a consultant may recommend that you purchase works by a certain artist, because the consultant owns a collection of works by that artist and wants to drive prices up. A collector of lunch boxes developed a market for his collection by writing and publishing a book on the qualities of this collectible. Once this book hit the market, prices soared. This phenomenon has occurred with many collectibles, so care should be taken when selecting your expert and conducting your research.

There are several other investment factors you should consider before purchasing any item. Collateral costs, such as the costs of maintenance, insurance, security systems, and proper air conditioning and humidity controls, should be estimated, although you may be able to reduce these costs by loaning an item or collection for display. Tax consequences of a later sale should also be considered if you anticipate reselling the item at a profit. You should also contemplate on other economic factors, such as resale royalties.

Financing Investments

One way of financing investment in collectibles is buying on installment. This method of purchasing is available in nearly every gallery in the United States, though it may not always be available for modestly priced collectibles, and is almost never a possibility when buying at garage sales or flea markets. Some investors use installment buying just as they would margin-buying on the stock market; their motive is quick profit from the resale of an object as soon as its price rises sufficiently.

Another method of financing collectibles is taking out a loan, using an item or the collection as collateral. While few banks are willing to lend money for the purchase of art, antiques, or other collectibles, some commentators estimate the combined credit available to collectors and dealers in the United States and Western Europe to be billions of dollars. The major lenders for art and other collectibles include Citibank, Rosenthal & Rosenthal, Chase Manhattan Bank, IBJ Schroder, and Sotheby's. Such financing programs are often combined with advisory services.

Auctions around the world saw success and record prices in the 1980s. There was a significant decline in the early 1990s, with a dramatic upsurge as the technology explosion occurred during the late 1990s, and, when the technology and dot.com bubble burst in the beginning of the 21st century, the art, antiques and collectibles market dropped, as well. Curiously, online sales continued to increase, both in quantity and price, though at a slower pace once the disposable income of the dot.com generation shrank. There are anomalies that continued to surface throughout this period. Record sales of certain items were announced in early 2002, despite the fact that the financial community indicated that a recession was in place.

CHAPTER 8

Conservation and Restoration

In order to protect your investments, as well as to ensure the availability of your works to future generations, you should be certain to correctly display and care for your collection.

Conservation is limited to protecting works from deterioration, while *restoration* is the act of reconstructing a work to its original state or condition. Conservation includes, for example, proper display and storage of works, cleaning, revarnishing oil paintings, and arresting bronze disease.

Suggested Methods of Display

In order to keep your collection in good condition, you must display it properly. The greatest protection you can provide for your collection is keeping its environment constant. Wide fluctuations of temperature and humidity may cause extensive damage to your collection. Excessive humidity can cause varnishes to turn opaque, the surfaces of works on paper to become dotted with brownish stains, and metals to rust. Humidity also causes *bronze disease*, which begins as bright green spots that spread rapidly and erodes bronze, brass and copper. This disease is contagious. Plastics are vulnerable to temperature fluctuation. They can melt, crack and discolor.

Temperatures should be maintained at 65º to 75ºF. through heating and air conditioning. The relative humidity should be 50% to 65% and can be controlled with humidifiers and dehumidifiers. Valuable collectibles generally should not be mounted against outside walls, in a kitchen or bathroom, or over radiators, heat vents, or a fireplace.

Paintings and works on paper should be exposed to as little light as possible, since unfiltered light causes discoloration and fading. Do not display valuable collectibles in direct sunlight or under fluorescent light. Fragile works can be covered by curtains, to be opened only for viewing the work. Works should be rotated periodically to prevent them from getting constant exposure to light from the same angle.

Airborne pollutants also cause damage. Proper framing can help protect paintings and works on paper. You should contact a museum or gallery for the names of reputable framers, since many framers are not knowledgeable about the special requirements for preserving these types of items. In addition, there are a number of professional framers' associations. Framers' yellow page ads typically identify professional affiliations, and you may be able to identify qualified framers in your local area by searching online. (See Chapter 13 for a discussion of framers' potential liability.)

Works on paper should be matted and framed behind glass or plexiglass. The mats protect the back of the work and prevent the glass from touching the work's surface. All mats and cardboard should be acid-free, and preferably of four-ply or eight-ply thickness.

Wood products made with formaldehyde, such as plywood, should not be used as frames, as the fumes can damage paint and paper. Many unprocessed woods contain a naturally-occurring chemical which causes yellowing of paper. If any type of wooden frame is used, it should be sealed with a special resin to isolate the work.

Pressure-sensitive tapes, such as cellophane and similar tapes, rubber cement, masking tape, paper tape, strapping tape, and synthetic glues should never be used to attach two-dimensional works to their mats. Works on paper should be attached with gummed paper or Japanese paper and starch paste. Photographs should be attached with Japanese paper and starch paste or be dry-mounted.

Paintings on wood should be framed somewhat loosely to allow for expansion. There should be room for a knife blade to pass between the edge of the wood and the frame.

Paintings on canvas should be backed with cardboard, with two-inch holes in the cardboard to allow for air circulation. They should also be hung so that air can circulate behind them. Attaching felt near the two bottom corners of the back of the frame will keep air from being trapped by the frame's bottom edge. Paintings should, of course, be hung securely so that there is no danger of falling.

Sculptures should be mounted on sturdy bases to prevent toppling. Cases can be used to protect fragile works. Outdoor sculptures may be particularly difficult to maintain, since they are exposed to the elements. Owners of outdoor sculptures should ask a conservator to design a maintenance program that includes annual inspections.

Another way to protect your collection is to rotate pieces. Display only a portion of your collection at one time, storing the rest under conditions that minimize exposure to light, dust, pollution, and fluctuations in temperature and humidity.

Two-dimensional works should be stored on sliding screens, or in a series of wooden or metal slots, with works separated by rigid sheets of strong cardboard. Works on paper should be stored in Solander boxes, made specifically for the purpose, or in metal storage drawers. They should be unframed but matted, and covered with a thin sheet of cellulose acetate (not suitable for pastels and charcoals) or Mylar. You should, however, never remove a professionally framed work from its frame. For long-term storage, use acid-free lining paper or Japanese vegetable paper. If mold should develop, dishes of thymol—a fungicide—can be used to kill it. Store the work in a closed container with the thymol for two to three days, with a 40-watt incandescent light bulb.

Prevention is certainly the preferred method of preserving works, because getting a deteriorating piece back to pristine condition is expensive and may even be impossible.

Signs of Deterioration

You should carefully monitor your works for any changes in condition. When examining paintings, look for surface ripples and bulges, age cracks, and flaking paint. Discoloration, fading, brittleness and disintegration are danger signs for plastics and works on paper. Bright green spots on bronze, brass or copper works are likely a sign of bronze disease. Porous items, such as ivory and wood, are vulnerable to mold and cracking. There are times when the services of a professional conservator are required.

Professional Conservators

Owners of valuable collections should have a conservator survey their collections periodically to point out any cleaning or restoration that needs to be done and to advise on the display of the collection. Conservators should be engaged for cleaning or other restoration of valuable works, as such work must be done by professionals in order to protect the item.

Choosing a qualified conservator is crucial. Contact a museum or gallery with a collection or specialty similar to yours, and ask for a recommendation. You can also contact the American Institute for Conservation of Historic and Artistic Works (AIC) (see Appendix A) for a list of member conservators in your area specializing in the kinds of works in your collection category. The AIC also offers a pamphlet called *Guidelines on Choosing a Conservator*. Again, the Yellow Pages and the Internet are good sources of information.

You should ask the conservator where he or she went to school and received other training, as well as how long he or she has been in the profession. Ask for other clients you may contact for a reference. Be sure the conservator is a member of the AIC. Although membership does not guarantee competence, certain training and experience standards must be met before membership is granted. Members also must pledge to abide by AIC's standards of professional conduct.

According to AIC, conservators should compile detailed records and reports on their progress and findings, and provide copies to the collector. An examination report should document the problems found, and a proposal for treatment should outline how the conservator intends to correct them. At this point, the conservator should estimate how long the treatment will take and the estimated cost. Conservators may charge by the hour, by the inch, or by the value of the work.

A report of treatment should detail the exact methods and materials used and should be accompanied by *before* and *after* photographs, as well as a photograph showing the *stripped down* work (cleaned of dirt, varnish and paint from previous restorations).

Conservation and Restoration Techniques

While collectors may be tempted to do simple conservation themselves, anything other than a light dusting (with a soft-bristled brush) of a valuable painting, sculpture or other collectible should be done by professionals. Never remove the patina from an item. This will likely reduce its value. An exception to this general rule is removing tarnish from gold or silver. If, however, the gold or silver is in the form of coins or medals then the tarnish should not be removed because the value could be affected. In addition, care should be taken when removing tarnish from gold or silver plate since the coatings may be quite thin. Aggressive tarnish removal could result in damage to the plating.

Varnish will probably need to be replaced every twenty to thirty years. A professional conservator will clean a painting using various chemicals, chosen according to the type of pigments used on the painting, to remove the old varnish. If the wrong chemicals are used, or the chemicals are left on too long, the pigment could be destroyed. A new coat of varnish is then applied.

Inpainting involves repainting the damaged areas of a canvas. First, the damaged area is sprayed with a thin coat of varnish, then the depression is filled in with gesso. After smoothing the gesso, another thin layer of varnish is applied. Finally, the painting is done, not with brush strokes, but with microscopic dots, to restore the original color and character intended by the artist. The surrounding area should not be overpainted.

Because the future may bring new and better conservation techniques, all treatments should be reversible.

When a canvas is torn or loose, relining is used to conserve it. A new canvas is bonded to the back of the old, using glue or wax.

Whether it is appropriate for a collector to have a work restored is a hotly contested issue. For some, restoration is important so that the appearance of the work will more closely resemble that which the creator intended. For others, restoration work performed by anyone other than the original creator is inappropriate and akin to creating a misleading item.

The debate surrounding the restoration of the Sistine Chapel continues to plague the art world. Since it is impossible to determine how Michelangelo's creation appeared when first completed, many feel that the stripping, cleaning, and repainting is inappropriate. Others appreciate the more vibrant appearance of the work and believe that it is more likely what the artist intended. One can speculate about the pros and cons with respect to virtually every form of restoration or correction, yet the choice is to be made by the collector.

If restoration is to be performed, it is most desirable to have the original creator do the work, if possible. Of course, this is impossible for antiquities or for works that need restoration after the creator's death or disability.

Acquisition of your collection requires the utmost care and skill, yet that is only part of the story. In order to preserve the work you have obtained, it is essential to employ proper conservation techniques and, if desired, restoration, as well. Owning a valuable work that has deteriorated is akin to abandoning your investment.

SECTION 2

Specific Legal Issues

The material that follows is intended to provide the reader with an analysis of some specific legal issues which should be considered when dealing with art, antiquities, and other collectibles. This chapter focuses on the copyright laws and identifies the rights to creative works. This is important, since the owner of a copyright in a work must generally expressly grant permission to allow the work to be reproduced.

In some jurisdictions, creative people have additional rights with respect to the work they create. This unique relationship between a work of art and the person who created it, known as the *droit moral* or *moral rights*, was first developed in Europe and is now part of American law as well. In addition, some jurisdictions provide creative people with the right to participate in the future enhanced value of their work when it is resold. It is important for purchasers to be aware of this right and to determine its applicability when acquiring a work.

The United States tax law is pervasive, and it, too, should be considered when dealing in art, antiquities, and other collectibles. Most states also have tax laws that may also apply to transactions in arts, antiquities and other collectibles.

It is important to determine whether there are any economic or legal restrictions on the movement of art, antiquities, or other collectibles across international borders. Failure to do so could be catastrophic and might subject violators to both civil and criminal penalties.

Not every one of the issues considered in these chapters will affect each transaction, but, nevertheless, prudence dictates that those who deal in art, antiquities, and other collectibles should be familiar with the laws and take steps to comply with them. What you do not know can, indeed, hurt you.

CHAPTER 9

Copyright

Collectors should be concerned with the complex legal rules of copyright, since these rules may determine some of their rights with respect to the works in their collections. Copyright is a bundle of rights generally given to creative people, including artists, photographers, craftspeople, and the like. These rights, granted by the federal copyright statute, concern the display, sale, and reproduction of creative works.

Copyright Act of 1976

Copyright is exactly what it claims to be—the right to make copies. Those rights are covered by various statutes, but the main body of law governing copyright is the Copyright Revision Act of 1976. This Act covers all works that were created on or after its effective date—January 1, 1978—and some aspects of works created earlier. While the pre-existing federal copyright law determines the copyright in works made before that date, the vast majority of contemporary works in your collection will likely be covered by the 1976 Act. In addition, some state laws deal with certain aspects of copyright. There are three multinational treaties that, in essence, provide reciprocal copyright protection in ninety-five countries with similar copyright laws.

Copyright encompasses five exclusive rights.

Right to Reproduce a Work by Any Means

In general, someone who reproduces a protected work without permission of the copyright owner infringes the copyright, whether the reproduction is made for commercial or non-commercial purposes, whether it is made for public distribution or private use, or whether many or only one reproduction is made. This means that, without permission of the copyright owner, you may not photograph protected works in your own collection, even for use on your holiday greeting cards. You may, however, reproduce protected works without permission if such reproduction involves *fair use*. (This is a very narrow exception to the copyright owner's rights and will be explained later in this chapter.)

RIGHT TO PREPARE DERIVATIVE WORKS BASED ON THE COPYRIGHTED WORK

A *derivative work* is one that transforms or adapts the subject matter of one or more preexisting works. Only the copyright owner, therefore, has the right to produce a poster bearing the image of a copyrighted piece of sculpture or to create a collage using all or part of a copyrighted work.

RIGHT TO DISTRIBUTE COPIES TO THE PUBLIC FOR SALE OR LEASE

Once the copyright owner sells a copy of the work or permits unrestricted distribution of that copy, however, the right to control the further use of that particular copy of the work usually ends. This is known as the *first sale doctrine*, and does not attach prior to the first sale if the work is merely in the possession of someone else temporarily—as in a rental—or if the copyright owner has an agreement with the purchaser restricting the purchaser's freedom to use the work. Under the first sale doctrine, a collector who has acquired a work without restriction is free to resell or lease that work.

RIGHT TO PERFORM A WORK PUBLICLY WHERE APPROPRIATE

This would not apply to works of visual art, and is most relevant for music, choreography, dramatic and audio-visual works, including movies, plays, and videos.

RIGHT TO DISPLAY THE WORK PUBLICLY

Once the copyright owner has sold a copy of the work, the purchaser has the right to display that copy. Those who borrow or rent the work, however, do not, in the absence of express authorization from the owner of the work or copyright in the work, have a right to display it. Thus, when collectors loan works to museums for exhibition, the loan agreement should have a clause specifically authorizing the museum to display the work.

Copyright Protection

Congress grants copyright protection to "original works of authorship fixed in any tangible medium of expression." Originality—as distinguished from uniqueness—requires that a work be created independently, but does not require that it be one-of-a-kind.

Functional art, such as rugs, clothing, and the like, is copyrightable only where the aesthetics of the work can exist separately from and be identified independently of the functionality of the work. In that situation, the aesthetic portion of the work is copyrightable. For example, potters have obtained copyrights for the surface designs of their pottery, but not for the pottery itself.

Compilations are also copyrightable, as long as the preexisting materials are gathered and arranged in a new or original form. Compilations such as collages or collaborations can be copyrightable as a whole, even though the contributions may also be separately copyrighted.

Purely functional works, such as collectible kitchen gadgets or the like, are not copyrightable. The protection afforded them may be under the patent laws, though no valid patent can be applied for if the invention has been *on sale* more than twelve months after it was invented. It is worth noting that patents are valid for twenty years from the date the application was filed. Few collectors would try to replicate patented inventions in their collections.

All copyrightable works are automatically protected by the federal copyright law as soon as they are fixed in a tangible medium, without the formal requirements of registration or deposit of copies. Registering the work, however, affords important and additional rights to the owner.

REGISTRATION

Although copyright protection is automatic when an idea is "fixed in a tangible medium of expression," registration is required in order for the copyright to be enforced and in order to obtain certain remedies. The law specifies that the copyright owner cannot bring a lawsuit to enforce the copyright until it has been registered with the Copyright Office. (See Appendix A for its address and phone number.)

If the copyright was registered prior to an infringement, the copyright owner who prevails in litigation may be entitled to the additional remedies of attorneys' fees and statutory damages. If the copyright is registered after an infringement occurs, the owner's legal remedies are limited to injunctive relief and actual provable damages. If registration is made within three months of publication, the registration will be retroactive, as if made on the date of first publication.

COPYRIGHT NOTICE

Although the law allows the creative person copyright on works published without notice, a person who copies a work in good faith, relying on the omission of notice, is considered an innocent infringer. In this situation, the person whose work was copied may not be able to recover damages. In fact, a court might even allow the copier to continue copying the work. The law provides that if notice is used, however, an infringer cannot claim that the infringement was innocent.

A copyright notice has the following three elements:

> ✣ the word *copyright* (or any recognized abbreviation) or the international copyright symbol ©;
> ✣ the year of first publication (or, in the case of unpublished works, the year in which the work was completed); and,
> ✣ the name of the copyright owner. If there are several owners, one name is sufficient.

These elements may appear in any order as long as they are permanently attached to the work and in some reasonable proximity to one another.

Copyright Owner

As a general rule, the creator of a work owns the copyright in that work. Under the old copyright law (which still applies, to some extent, to works created before January 1, 1978), when a work was sold, ownership of the copyright passed to the purchaser unless the creator reserved it in a written agreement. New York and California changed this rule in 1976 by providing, in their state laws, that where an artist sold a work of art, it was presumed that the copyright in that work was retained by the artist unless there was a written contract stating otherwise. The Copyright Revision Act of 1976 adopted this position. For works that still have a valid copyright, you likely own that copyright if the work was purchased before January 1, 1978, though be sensitive to the New York and California changes where the purchase date is prior to 1976.

WORK FOR HIRE

The *work-for-hire* doctrine is an exception to the general rule that the artist owns the copyright in the work he or she has created. When a work is created by an employee within the scope of his or her employment, the copyright belongs to the employer. For example, the owner of a copyright in a sculpture created on campus by an art teacher may be the school. Thus, you would seek reproduction rights from the school, rather than from the artist.

Even works created by independent contractors may be *works for hire* if the work was

> → specially ordered or commissioned;
> → one of a specified class of works, i.e., a text, a test, answer material for a test, a translation, a supplement, a compilation, a movie or other audio-visual work, an atlas, or a contribution to a collective work; and,
> → the parties agree in writing that the work is to be a work for hire.

It is important for you to determine who owns the copyright in a work when you wish to photograph or otherwise reproduce it.

An experienced intellectual property lawyer can help you with this determination.

TRANSFERRING COPYRIGHT

A copyright owner may sell the entire copyright, assign any part of it, or permit the use of any part. The rights being sold, assigned, or licensed should be specifically identified and transferred through a written contract. While oral permission may be enforceable, sales or assignments of a copyright must be in writing. The contract should state the scope, duration, frequency of use, type of use, and any restrictions.

For example, if a collector is granted the right to photograph a painting and use the reproduction for Christmas cards, can the image also be used by the collector to make posters? The answer is no, unless the contract has also specified poster reproduction as a permitted use. A well-drafted contract will make it clear that no other use is permitted.

Assignments of copyright ownership and written licensing agreements may be recorded with the Copyright Office for an $80 registration fee for one title and $20 for additional titles in groups of ten. Before an assignee or a licensee can sue a third party for infringement, the document of transfer must be recorded.

Once the transaction has been recorded, the rights of the assignee or licensee are protected in much the same way as the rights of an owner of real estate are protected by recording the deed. In a case of conflicting transfers of rights, if both transactions are recorded within one month of the signing, the person whose transaction was completed first prevails. If the transactions are not recorded within a month of the execution, the one who records first prevails. A recorded non-exclusive license prevails over any unrecorded transfer of ownership.

You should be aware that the 1976 Copyright Act provides a copyright owner the right to terminate copyright transfers and licenses. For published works, the copyright proprietor may terminate the transfer or license thirty-five years after the date of transfer; for works unpublished at the time of transfer, the copyright owner may terminate the transfer or license thirty-five years from the date of publication. Publication is defined as the distribution of copies of a work to the public by sale or other transfer of ownership, or by rental, lease or loan. It does not occur when the work is displayed to a select group for a special purpose without the right of reproduction, distribution or sale.

Remember that what you believed to be an outright purchase of a copyright for its entire term may actually only be for a limited time period.

DURATION OF COPYRIGHT

Under the current law, copyright exists for the life of the creator plus seventy years. If the work is created jointly, the copyright expires seventy years after the last creator dies. The Copyright Office keeps records of famous authors' deaths as of the mid-1960s but, where the Office does not have records of deaths, they assume the author is dead ninety-five years after the first publication date or 120 years after creation, whichever occurs first. This also applies to composite, anonymous, and pseudonymous works. Works created before January 1, 1978 are protected seventy-five years from the date copyright was first obtained. In all cases, copyright terms end on December 31 of the relevant year.

PUBLIC DOMAIN

Once the copyright on a work has expired or been lost, the work enters the *public domain*, where it can be used for copyright purposes by anyone in any manner. This means, for example, that anyone—not just the owner of the copyright or of the work—may be free to reproduce the work in any medium.

Even though a work is in the public domain, and there are thus no copyright restrictions on copying, there may be other rights which inhibit reproduction of the work. Each person has a right of privacy in his or her image and an individual, during his or her lifetime, may prevent the unauthorized use of his or her image for most purposes. The same is true of an individual's name and identifiable reputation. Famous people who, themselves, exploit their notoriety—such as Elvis Presley, Marilyn Monroe, and James Dean—may have rights of publicity in their names, likeness and reputations which may even survive their deaths. It is for this reason that many entertainers and sports figures earn significant fees for their endorsements of products or services.

> *For example, it has been reported that Michael Jordan, during his last year as a basketball star with the Chicago Bulls, earned approximately $8 million from his basketball contract, but $30 million for product endorsements.*

There are other legal restrictions on the use of certain images, as well. For example, it is unlawful to reproduce U.S. currency, to misuse the image of the U.S. Forest Service's Smokey Bear, or to improperly reproduce certain certification marks. The *trademark laws* also inhibit the unauthorized use of names, symbols and logos when there is a likelihood that the unpermitted use will cause confusion by the public. It is even unlawful to photograph certain buildings, such as post offices, military installations, and the like.

A person can obtain copyright in the new aspects of a work derived from a work in the public domain. For example, Rembrandt's painting *Night Watch* cannot be copyrighted, but a photograph of it can. Consequently, no one would be able to copy that photograph without permission of the photographer, although anyone else would be able to copy Rembrandt's original. The photograph is a copyrightable *derivative work* of a preexisting work.

COPYRIGHT INFRINGEMENT AND REMEDIES

Copyright infringement occurs when an unauthorized person exercises any of the five exclusive rights which comprise copyright. The fact that the infringing party did not intend to improperly use protected rights or did not know that the work was protected is relevant only with respect to the severity of the penalty for infringement.

In the absence of an agreement to the contrary, a collector who does not own the copyright in a work may not reproduce the work or create derivatives of the work—to do so is infringement.

A collector who owns the copyright in a particular work has the right to enforce that copyright against others, including the artist who created the work. The artist may be liable as an infringer if a subsequent work by that artist is copied from the earlier work. A mere similarity in style or subject matter is not enough to establish infringement, however.

One who resells an infringing work is also an infringer, even if that person did not produce the infringing work. This applies even where the individual acquires the work overseas and imports it into the

United States. You should, therefore, be careful when reselling recently created works of uncertain provenance.

All actions for infringement of copyright must be brought in a federal court within three years of the date of the infringement. The complainant must prove that the work was copyrighted and registered, that the infringer had access to and copied the protected work, and that the infringer copied a *substantial and material* portion of the copyrighted work. In order to demonstrate the extent of the damage caused by the infringement, the copyright owner must also provide evidence that shows how widely the infringing copies were distributed.

The copyright owner must prove that the infringer had access to the protected work, because an independent creation of an identical work is not an infringement. Thus, if, by coincidence, two individuals create works that are *substantially similar,* or even identical, and neither copies from the other, then neither work is an infringing work and neither creator is an infringer of the other's work. Infringement can occur, however, even if an entire work was not copied, because any unauthorized copying of a substantial portion of a work constitutes infringement.

If the expressions of ideas, rather than simply the ideas alone, are found to be similar, the court must decide whether the similarity is substantial and whether the work itself is copyrighted. This is done in two steps. First, the court looks at the more general similarities of the works, such as subject matter, setting, materials used, and the like. The second step involves a subjective judgment of the works' intrinsic similarity: Would a lay observer recognize that the alleged copy had been appropriated from the copyrighted work?

If the work is held to be an infringement, the court can order the destruction of all copies and enjoin future infringement. In addition, the copyright owner may be awarded damages. The copyright owner may request that the court award *actual damages* or, if the work was registered prior to the infringement, *statutory damages*—a choice that can be made any time before the final judgment is entered.

Actual damages are either the amount of the financial injury sustained by the copyright owner (or assignee or licensee) or the equivalent of the profits made by the infringer. In proving the infringer's profits, the copyright owner need only establish the gross revenues received. The infringer then may prove any legally deductible expenses.

The amount of statutory damages is decided by the court, within specified limits: no less than $750 and no more than $30,000. The maximum possible recovery is increased to $150,000 if the copyright owner proves that the infringement was willful. The court has the option to award the prevailing party its costs and attorneys' fees, provided the copyright was registered prior to the infringement.

The U.S. Department of Justice can also criminally prosecute a copyright infringer. If the prosecutor proves beyond a reasonable doubt that the infringement was committed willfully and for commercial gain, the infringer can be fined and sentenced to jail. A number of individuals have been imprisoned for large-scale copyright infringements.

FAIR USE

Not every copying of a protected work is an actionable infringement. The copyright statute recognizes that copies of a protected work "for purposes such as criticism, comment, news reporting, teaching (including multiple copies for classroom use), scholarship or research" can be considered fair use and, therefore, not actionable. This is not, however, a complete list nor is it intended as a definition of *fair use*. In fact, fair use is not defined by the statute. Instead, the law cites four criteria to be considered in determining whether a particular use is or is not fair:

→ the purpose and character of the use, including whether it is for commercial gain or for nonprofit educational purposes;

→ the nature of the copyrighted work;

→ the amount and substantiality of the portion used in relation to the copyrighted work as a whole; and,

→ the effect of the use upon the potential market for, or value of, the copyrighted work.

The law does not rank these four criteria, nor does it exclude other factors in determining a use is fair. All the law does is leave the doctrine of fair use to be further developed by the courts.

Publishing in a catalog a photo of a work to be sold at auction would likely be considered fair use. A collector probably can photograph copyrighted works for insurance purposes, or as the backdrop for a family portrait which will not be reproduced. It is likely fair use when a copyrighted work appears in a magazine, such as *Architectural Digest*, when the work is merely incidental to a photo of a collector's home.

Without permission, a collector probably may not reproduce a copyrighted work for use on posters or greeting cards, since this would be a commercial use and would likely affect the copyright owner's market in reproduction rights.

This discussion points out that it is not easy to define what sorts of uses are *fair* uses. Questions continue to be resolved on a case-by-case basis. You should consult with an experienced copyright attorney if you intend to use someone else's copyrighted work without permission.

Conclusion

It is important to remember that the copyright laws of the United States are extremely complex and are frequently amended. It is, thus, essential for anyone involved with copyright issues to work with an experienced copyright lawyer in order to avoid the myriad problems which can and do arise in

The mere fact that you own a copy-righted work does not necessarily mean that you own the copyright in that work. The penalties for infringement are serious, and care should be taken to avoid violating intellectual property laws.

this field. The mere fact that you own a copyrighted work does not necessarily mean that you own the copyright in that work. The penalties
for infringement are serious, and care should be taken to avoid violating intellectual property laws.

CHAPTER 10

When Rights Collide

Collectors should be aware that artists have certain rights in their works which are unique to works of art. Artists have an interest in deciding whether to release their works, seeing that their creations retain the form they gave them, and ensuring that the artists are credited with the works' creation. Because these rights affect the artist and are intertwined with the artist's personality, they are known as *moral rights*, or *droit moral*. These moral rights given to the artist limit a collector's rights in the works purchased. You should, therefore, be familiar with these rights and the types of works affected.

Moral Rights

Droit moral, which originated in France, is now recognized in eighty-one countries throughout the world. While moral rights are often thought to conflict with the property rights of owners in the U.S., protection of certain moral rights became mandatory when the United States became a party to a treaty known as the Berne Convention in 1988.

Partially as a result, Congress passed the Visual Artists Rights Act (VARA), which provides to *authors* of certain artwork the rights of attribution and integrity. VARA applies only to one-of-a-kind or limited editions (signed and consecutively numbered) of 200 or fewer paintings, drawings, prints, and sculptures. Photographs are covered if they are produced for exhibition purposes only in editions of 200 or fewer. Penalties for violation of VARA include all those for copyright infringement, except criminal sanctions. The moral rights granted by VARA may be waived by the artist, but not transferred.

The moral rights granted by VARA only affect works by living artists.

A collector seeking a waiver of these rights by the artist should be certain to get the waiver in writing. The writing must specify the identity of the work and rights being waived and be signed by the artist. For a joint work, a waiver by one of the artists is deemed to be a waiver for all of the artists.

THE RIGHT TO CREATE

One of the rights included in the droit moral is the right to create or to refraining from creating. An artist's ability to be the sole judge of whether his or her work is ready to be displayed is the protection of the right to create. For instance, if an artist has agreed under contract to produce a specific work for you and does not, can you sue to require its creation or completion?

In the United States, an artist's or craftsperson's right to create is protected because they will not be forced to compute contracts for personal services. In legal terms, these types of contracts are not specifically enforceable. There are several reasons for this rule. First, it is difficult to force or to gauge the quality of the work done. Second, it is rarely desirable to require parties to work closely together after disputes have arisen and confidence and loyalty destroyed. Finally, requiring the creative person to work is inconsistent with the constitutional prohibition against involuntary servitude.

So, while you can sue the creative person for breach of contract, you will not be able to force creation or completion of the work. The breaching creative person may still be held liable for damages, however. Courts may also prohibit the creative person from working for others on comparable projects during the term of the contract with you.

THE RIGHT OF DISCLOSURE

This right allows an artist or craftsperson to prevent someone else from publishing a work that the creative person has discarded. For example, if you buy a work which turns out to have been acquired from the creative person's trash, you will have no right to display that work. In the United States, this right may be protected by the constitutional right of privacy and by the copyright law since the creator has the exclusive right to exploit his or her work.

THE RIGHT TO WITHDRAW

The right to withdraw a work after it has been disclosed is not recognized in the United States. For example, one court held that an actor could not cause the withdrawal of a film of his work, even though he felt that the film injured his reputation due to its inferior quality. Furthermore, under the copyright law, the owner of a lawfully made copy of a work has the unqualified right to display that copy publicly and to sell or otherwise dispose of that copy. This means that if you own an early work which the creator claims injures his or her current reputation, you may continue to display that work.

NAME ATTRIBUTION

VARA allows an artist to claim authorship of a work he or she created. The artist also has the right to prevent the use of his or her name as the creator of the work if the work has been distorted, mutilated, or otherwise modified so as to injure the artist's honor or reputation. So, if a work in your collection has been modified, the artist may require removal of his or her name from the work. While Massachusetts and New Mexico laws provide a right to *pseudonymity* (the use of a fictitious name), VARA does not.

Artists and craftspeople also are protected from false attribution by the right of privacy, the doctrine of unfair competition and the doctrine of defamation. By contrast, artists and craftspeople ordinarily may not object to the use of their names in a truthful statement that they created the works or that the works are based on or derived from their works. You are, thus, free to attribute a work to the artist or craftsperson who created it. Creators ordinarily may not object to the omission of their names either, unless the work is covered by VARA or a state law. California and New York provide that an artist who creates an original painting, sculpture or drawing retains the right to claim authorship, even after the work is sold.

INTEGRITY

Artists also have some rights to prevent their works from being altered, distorted, or destroyed. VARA affords artists the right to prevent intentional distortions, mutilations, or other modifications. VARA does not prohibit modifications resulting from passage of time or modifications that are the result of conservation or presentation (including lighting and placement) unless gross negligence caused the modification.

This means that if, for example, your lighting of a work has caused it to fade, you will not be liable to the artist unless you were grossly negligent. You have no right, however, to remove parts of a sculpture so that it will fit in the space you intended, or even to display singly pieces from a composite work, like one-third of a triptych. You may not, for instance, colorize a drawing or permanently remove or cover a part you dislike of a painting, if the work is protected by VARA.

VARA also provides the artist the right to prevent the destruction of a work of recognized stature. Thus, you may not be allowed to burn that portrait of your ex-spouse. The question of what constitutes a work of recognized stature must be determined by scholars, curators and, presumably, collectors.

Several states also have enacted statutes that protect the right of integrity. These are California, Connecticut, Louisiana, Maine, Massachusetts, Nevada, New Mexico, New York, Pennsylvania, Rhode Island, and Utah. Where state legislation and VARA are unavailable, the right to privacy and doctrine of unfair competition may provide some rights to the creator. Thus, you should contact an art lawyer before modifying the work of any living artist or craftsperson.

EXCESSIVE CRITICISM

A final moral right is the right to be protected from excessive criticism. While the right to freedom of speech demands that critics be allowed to express their opinions, when criticism amounts to an unwarranted, abusive attack on the creator or his or her work, it may violate the creator's personal rights. There is really no remedy for excessive criticism in the United States, since libel actions will be successful only where the creator's reputation is unjustifiably attacked.

Resale Royalties

There may be specific legal and contractual obligations imposed on the seller when reselling artwork. In Europe, the law often requires those who resell art to pay a certain amount from the resale to the artist or the artist's estate. The amount of this payment—called a *resale royalty* or *droit de suite*—varies from country to country.

The United States does not yet have a national resale royalties law. California has the only statewide resale royalties statute. It provides that, whenever a work of fine art is resold and the seller lives in California or the sale takes place in California, the seller must pay 5% of the amount of the sales price to the artist or to the artist's estate.

For the purposes of this statute, an artist is defined as the person who created the art and who, at the time of resale, either is a citizen of the United States or has resided in California for a minimum of two years. Fine art is defined as an original painting, sculpture, or drawing, or an original work of art in glass.

The law does not apply to the initial sale of a work, to the resale of a work for a gross sales price of less than $1,000, or to the resale of the work for a gross sales price less than the purchase price paid by the seller. The law also excludes sales that occur more than twenty years after the artist's death, resales of works by an art dealer to a purchaser within ten years of the initial sale of the work by the artist to the dealer, provided all intervening sales are between dealers, and sales of stained glass where the work has been permanently attached to a building and is sold as part of the sale of that building. This law also applies to Internet sales where the sale is initiated from California.

Generally, the responsibility for paying the artist is with the seller. If you sell the work at an auction or through a gallery, dealer, broker, museum or other person acting as your agent, however, the agent must withhold the 5% and locate and pay the artist or the artist's estate. If the artist cannot be located within ninety days, the royalty is transferred to the California State Arts Council. If the Arts Council cannot locate the artist, and if the artist does not file a written claim for the money within seven years from the date of the sale, the Arts Council may use the money to acquire art for its Art in Public Places program.

Remember that, even where you personally do not have the responsibility of locating the artist, that 5% royalty will decrease the amount of money you receive when reselling artwork. When selling any work from your collection, determine whether you have any resale royalty obligations.

Many artists and craftspeople have established their own resale royalty arrangement by contractually requiring purchasers to pay a specified amount should the purchaser resell the work.

Check local laws, as well as your contract with the creator or dealer from whom you purchased the work, and any prior contracts they may have had regarding the piece, to determine whether you may have some ongoing financial obligation to the creator or his or her estate.

CHAPTER 11

Tax Considerations

There may be tax consequences associated with buying, maintaining, selling, and/or making a gift of a work of art, antique, or other collectible. A collector should be concerned with and be sensitive to these issues. These transactions may be taxed under the income tax, gift tax, and/or estate tax laws. Different tax rates are applicable, depending on how the transaction is structured. Effective planning may minimize your tax liability.

Income Tax

The first step in determining income tax is identifying gross income, defined as "all income from whatever source derived." This is a broad definition, and it includes gains from the sale of property.

The amount of gain realized on the sale of a work of art, antique or other collectible is calculated by subtracting the seller's basis in the item from the price received from the sale of it. Usually, the basis is the amount you originally spent to purchase the work. If, however, it was acquired as a gift, your basis will be the same as the donor's basis. If it was bequeathed, then your basis will be the fair market value of the work at the time of the giver's death or date selected for valuing the estate.

With these and a few other exceptions, gain realized can be loosely thought of as profit on resale.

Usually, the amount of gain realized is to be recognized, which means that the gain must be included as part of your gross income.

CAPITAL GAINS

Once gain is recognized, it is taxable. The rate of tax is determined by whether the gain is characterized as ordinary income or capital gain, and whether the capital gain is long term or short-term. If you held the asset for more than one year before you disposed of it, your capital gain is long term. If you held it one year or less, your capital gain is short term. Long term capital gains may be taxed at a much lower rate than ordinary income.

A *capital asset* is an asset other than inventory. Dealers, who are systematically engaged in buying and selling art, antiques and other collectibles, cannot characterize their income as capital gains, since the sale of inventory creates ordinary income. Collectors, however, generally do characterize income from the sale of works in their collections as capital gain.

DEDUCTIONS

After characterizing your income, you must determine how much of it is taxable. You are permitted to deduct certain business expenses in order to calculate adjusted gross income. Other itemized deductions are subtracted from adjusted gross income in order to determine taxable income.

There are two categories of deductible expenses potentially available to collectors: expenses for the production of income and business expenses. Collectors may deduct expenses of maintaining and reselling works in their collections, such as conservation and commission costs, but only up to the amount received from sales of works in their collections. If you report no income from the sale, rental or reproduction of works in your collection, you can take no deductions for maintenance of your collection.

In order to be deductible against income from other activities, an expense must be incurred in connection with a business or investment activity, rather than for personal reasons. Because collecting may also be a hobby, it is often difficult for collectors to prove that investment is their primary reason for collecting.

Having an investment purpose alone will not remove your collecting activity from being a hobby. To do that, investment must be your primary motive. One case held that expenses related to acquiring and maintaining a sizeable art collection were not deductible against income from other activities. Although there was evidence that the taxpayers invested in art because they were wary of other investments, that they kept meticulous records of their art business activities, and that much of their time was spent away from the residences in which most of the art was stored, the court focused on the facts that a great deal of the taxpayers' personal lives revolved around their art collection and collecting activities and that they made extensive personal use of their collection.

There is, however, a presumption that your collection is an investment if you reported a profit from this activity in at least three of the past five years.

In addition to showing that an expense was not incurred for personal reasons, you must show that the expense is ordinary and necessary and that it is a current expense rather than a capital investment. The ordinary and necessary requirement is met by most reasonable expenses, and includes a statutory percentage of traveling expenses and lodging on business trips. Current expenses are those that create benefits only in the current tax year.

Deductions for the purchase of property, not held as business inventory, whose useful life extends substantially beyond the close of the tax year are not allowed. These are capital investments, not current expenses. The deduction for the cost of these items must be spread over the theoretical useful life of the property, instead of being taken in the year of purchase. This is known as *depreciation*. For example, the costs of installation of heat and humidity controls in a building for conservation purposes cannot be deducted as a current expense, but are added to the taxpayer's basis in the building and then amortized over time. Simple repairs and maintenance, such as repairing a chipped frame on a painting or re-gluing an antique chair, are deductible as current expenses.

Since most works of art, antiques and other collectibles do not decline in quality or become obsolete, they do not have a limited useful life. A mere decline in value of a work does not entitle the owner to a depreciation deduction. This means, for instance, that a business using artwork to decorate its offices may not take depreciation deductions for the artwork, although other office furnishings and decorations may be depreciable. Similarly, a collector who decorates his or her home with a collection of Mickey Mouse items cannot take a depreciation deduction if the famous rodent declines in popularity and value.

LOSSES

You may deduct any loss incurred in a business or investment activity or as a result of casualty (fire, storm, etc.) or theft. If a work of art, antique or collectible is considered a capital asset and is sold for a price which is lower than the price you paid or your other basis in the item, you may be able to claim the difference between what your basis is in the piece and the amount for which you resold it as a capital loss. This is especially important where, for example, you innocently purchase an object that you later discover is a worthless forgery. This type of loss deduction is available only to offset your capital gains derived from your collection, unless you are able to establish that you purchased the work primarily as an investment, rather than merely for personal enjoyment.

Capital losses are first used to offset capital gains in the year incurred. Any additional capital losses incurred in a business or investment activity are deductible from ordinary income up to a maximum amount of $3,000 per year, or $1,500 if you are married and filing a separate tax return. Any excess loss can be carried forward to the following tax year.

You may be able to deduct large casualty losses, whether or not they occur in connection with a business or investment activity. If an item is stolen, damaged or destroyed and you are not compensated for the loss (by insurance or otherwise), you may deduct the entire amount of the loss except for the first $100, to the extent that this and other casualty losses exceed 10% of your adjusted gross income.

For example, if your adjusted gross income is $300,000, and your
casualty loss is $50,100, you may deduct $20,000:
$50,100 - 100 = $50,000
$300,000 x 10% = $30,000
$50,000 - $30,000 = $20,000

On the other hand, if you do receive insurance proceeds as the result of a casualty loss and the property was insured for an amount greater than your basis, you may elect not to recognize the gain, so long as you reinvest the insurance proceeds in similar property within two tax years of the loss. This means you will not pay tax on the gain until you sell (or otherwise dispose of) the newly acquired item.

CHARITABLE CONTRIBUTIONS

You may be able to take a deduction from adjusted gross income for items that you donate to certain qualified charitable organizations. The amount of such deductions is subject to certain percentage limitations. Contributors of capital gain property, such as artwork, antiques and collectibles, are limited to a 30% deduction for contributions to churches, governmental units, educational organizations and certain other organizations, and 20% for contributions made to other charities.

Under the alternative minimum tax provisions (which limit deductions for certain taxpayers), appreciated property donated to charity is treated as a tax preference, with certain exceptions to encourage donation of art, antiques and collectibles to museums, galleries, libraries and public collections by allowing collectors to deduct the fair market value of their donations, rather than the basis.

Some types of contributions are not deductible. No charitable deduction is allowed for the value of services, although out-of-pocket expenses incurred in performing the services can be deducted.

A gift of a future interest in tangible personal property is deductible only after all intervening interests in the property either have expired or are held by someone other than the donor (or the donor's family). For example, you might donate an antique table to a museum today, while reserving the right to retain possession of the item until your death. Although you would like to take a deduction while retaining possession of the work, you may not deduct your contribution until the museum takes possession of the table.

It is possible, however, to transfer a present interest in property while retaining an interest in the work and still be eligible for a charitable deduction. For example, you may contribute a present one-quarter interest in an antique silver charger, entitling the museum to possession during three months of each year. You could then keep the charger for the rest of the year, and would be entitled to a deduction for one-fourth of the work's value.

The amount of a particular charitable deduction is generally its fair market value. This may be reduced, depending on the character of the contributed property and its use by the recipient. If the donated item was held by the donor as inventory or for less than one year, or if the item is given to a private foundation or its use is unrelated to the recipient's charitable mission, then the deduction is limited to the donor's basis in the property.

Donations valued in excess of $5,000 must be substantiated by a qualified appraisal document prepared within sixty days of the donation. This document must include a description of the item, its physical condition, the date of contribution, the terms of any agreement concerning the item made by the donor and donee, the appraiser's name, address and qualifications, the date of appraisal, that the appraisal was made for tax purposes, the appraised value, the method of appraisal, and the basis used in determining value. The taxpayer may deduct the cost of appraisal fees as part of the charitable contribution. If the item is valued at $20,000 or more, there are more demanding requirements. Since the tax laws change frequently, you should consult a tax professional or visit Internal Revenue's website, www.irs.gov, in order to determine the rules in effect on the date of your donation.

An accurate appraisal is important because you may be assessed a penalty for *overvaluation*. The penalty applies if the value of the property as claimed on your return is 200% or more of its correctly determined value and the underpayment of tax attributable to the total of all overvaluations made by you for the tax year amounts to $5,000 or more. The amount of the penalty is 20% of the underpayment. A 40% penalty applies if the claimed property value is 400% or more of its true value. Thus, there are strong incentives for you to value as accurately as possible works donated to charities.

Valuation problems customarily fall into two general categories:

➔ either the appraiser and the IRS disagree on the value of the item or
➔ the authenticity of the item is questioned.

In order to resolve such problems, the IRS has established special panels to review the deductions taken by donors. These Advisory Panels typically recommend lowering the value for items claimed by taxpayers as charitable donations and increasing the values for items contained within decedents' estates. In addition, members of the panels may testify in court if a dispute over the valuation of an item arises.

Gift and Estate Considerations

The importance of planning the disposition of collections after the owner's death cannot be overemphasized. Collections present special problems not encountered with other kinds of personal property. A collection of a group of pieces may be more valuable if left intact, rather than being split up between several beneficiaries. Some beneficiaries may not want to own valuable items, because of their maintenance costs. Other beneficiaries may choose to keep an item, even though its monetary value is minimal.

The typical will bequeaths personal property to the surviving spouse or, if there is no surviving spouse, to the surviving children. Where the property passes to the decedent's spouse, there is an unlimited marital deduction for both estate and gift tax purposes. No tax will be owed unless the spouse sells the property in his or her lifetime for more than its value at the time of the decedent's death. If the property is not disposed of, it will be included in the spouse's estate at its fair market value at the date of the spouse's death or the alternative date selected for valuation of the spouse's estate.

In addition to being able to use the marital deduction, each individual is given a lifetime unified tax credit for gift tax liability. Any unused credit is applied to estate tax liability. This means that a certain amount of property may pass tax-free without using the marital deduction. In larger estates, it would be a mistake to leave the whole estate to the spouse and, therefore, lose this tax credit.

There are many other ways for you to reduce your estate tax liability. Charitable contributions reduce the amount of property left in your taxable estate and enable you to take an appropriate deduction for the value of the property donated. Non-charitable gifts made during your lifetime also reduce the size of your *estate*. The first $11,000 ($22,000 for married couples) of gifts to any one person in each tax year is excluded from gift tax liability. This amount can change with inflation.

Beyond this, there is no difference between gift tax and estate tax rates, so no real tax benefits to the collector (or the estate) will be realized by making a gift unless the property is expected to appreciate sub-stantially from the time of the gift to the time of the collector's death.

If the tax consequences to the recipient are also taken into account, however, it may be advantageous to leave appreciated prop-erty in the collector's estate and let the property pass to the recipient upon the collector's death. The recipient/beneficiary will then take the property with the higher fair-market-value basis, rather than the lower collector's basis. This will lessen the recipient's taxable gain if the property is later sold.

A collector should avoid certain types of gift transactions occur-ring within three years of his or her death, if the death can be antici-pated. If the *decedent* (or the decedent's spouse) has made gifts that required payment of gift taxes, within three years of death, the amount of each gift tax is added back into the gross estate. In addition, if the decedent transferred property in which he or she retained a life estate, or transferred the right to receive life insurance proceeds, then the value of the property transferred will be included in the gross estate. This also occurs if the transfer was revocable or taking effect only at the decedent's death.

The use of *trusts* can also be an attractive way of reducing estate tax liability. For estate tax purposes, property transferred into a properly structured trust will be excluded from your gross estate so long as you do not die within three years of the transfer and so long as you do not retain a pro-hibited interest in or power over the trust. For income tax purposes, income produced by the trust will be taxable to the trust (or, if distributed, to the beneficiaries of the trust), not to you.

Collectors should consult with their tax advisors, as well as an expert in estate planning, to determine the most appropriate method of struc-turing an art-, antique- or col-lectible-related transaction.

In addition, every well-drafted estate plan should address the collection in order to accomplish the collector's objectives while minimizing the estate's tax liabilities.

Since the tax laws are in constant flux, it is essential for you to work with a qualified tax professional or, at the very least, to check with the IRS and state taxing authorities with respect to the effect of contemplated transactions on your tax situation. The IRS maintains information hotlines, though opinions expressed through this service are not binding on the IRS. Consult the government pages in your local phone directory, or the IRS website, www.irs.gov, for the appropriate number. The IRS website also provides a wealth of other useful information, examples, and access to IRS forms and free publications.

CHAPTER 12

Import and Export Restrictions for the Collector

There are a number of issues you should consider before importing works into the United States for your collection. These include a determination of whether the item you desire to import has been lawfully exported, and the costs associated with importing the work. (See Appendix D for the FBI and Interpol websites, which discuss recent developments in this area and the myriad restrictions.) It is important to recognize the fact that even if you are bringing back a souvenir from a trip the same laws may apply. In today's world, carrying documentation of items acquired overseas is essential. It is also a good idea to be sure that the work can be easily unpacked or uncrated for inspection when entering the United States.

Customs Duties

Customs means duties, tolls or taxes imposed by a government on transactions across its borders. Customs is also the agency which administers the laws regulating these transactions.

Customs works in two directions, *import* and *export*. If an object being shipped out of this country will ultimately be returned—for example, a collection on loan to a museum—this should be noted on the export declaration so that the Customs officials will permit the item back into the country duty-free as *American goods returned*.

If you receive a shipment from another country, you will have to clear it through Customs. It is necessary to have the bill of lading and invoices to bring the shipment into the United States. For artworks and antiquities, you should also provide documentation showing the name of the artist and/or the time period when the item was created.

Import and export is a very specialized kind of activity. As a result, collectors should consider the use of professionals in these activities.

Freight forwarders who specialize in overseas shipments can handle the whole export operation. To clear an incoming shipment through Customs, a customshouse broker is often the most knowledgeable. These specialists are listed in most telephone book yellow pages and online. Freight forwarders can be found in cities that have major ports or international air terminals.

DUTY-FREE ENTRY FOR ART

Although customs duties are imposed on most commodities imported into the United States, including collectibles, antiques works of art may enter duty-free. It is, therefore, essential to determine what is *art* for customs purposes. The law in this area is quite complex, but there are some guidelines.

Only the artwork is duty-free. For instance, a painting will not be taxed, but its frame will be.

> ✦ In order for an item to qualify as duty-free fine art, it cannot be functional. Most crafts, therefore, do not qualify.
> ✦ The work must be created by an artist and cannot be imported for the purpose of commercialization—for example, you cannot import a duty-free painting to be used as cover art on a magazine.
> ✦ Fine art prints can enter duty-free only if they are hand-pulled from handmade plates.
> ✦ Only the first twelve pieces of limited edition sculpture can enter the United States as duty-free art.

FUNCTIONAL WORKS, SUCH AS CRAFTS, TOYS
AND OTHER COLLECTIBLES

Many items greatly valued by collectors do not fit within the Customs definition of art, and are, thus, generally subject to tariff duties. For example, because pottery and frames are functional, they do not qualify as art. Similarly, toys, dolls, action figures and the like, are also deemed functional and may be subject to tariff duties.

Some collectibles not meeting the Customs definition of art may still enter duty-free if they originate from a country with *Generalized System of Preference* (GSP) status. The GSP is a customs law enacted to provide certain underdeveloped countries with the ability to have some of their commodities enter the United States without the imposition of tariffs. The countries on the GSP list change quite regularly, as do the duty-free commodities. It is, therefore, essential for you to consult with a customs broker and/or an experienced art lawyer when contemplating overseas purchases. You might also check the Customs Service website, www.customs.gov.

You should obtain a certificate from a seller when you intend to rely on the GSP exemption. Many overseas dealers have printed certificates for this purpose. In more rural communities, you may have to prepare the documentation, which should contain at least the country of origin; the name of the creator, if known; the date the work was created, if known; the materials used; and any other significant information about the work, such as its possible use or significance to people creating it.

In addition to exemptions for items from GSP nations, there are certain tariff exemptions that apply to acquisitions made by tourists. Returning U.S. citizens may claim a $400 personal exemption on articles purchased abroad. The duty-free exemption is $600 if you are returning directly from a Caribbean Basin Economic Recovery Act country. The exemption is $1,200 if returning from American Samoa, Guam, or the U.S. Virgin Islands. The exemption is based on the retail value of an item in the country where it was purchased, and is allowed only where the item was acquired for personal use and obtained only as an incident to the trip. Furthermore, the item must be properly declared upon return to the United States and the trip abroad must have been of at least 48 hours in duration.

Exemptions from Duty for Antiquities and Certain Ethnographic Works

Antiquities, which are generally defined for Customs purposes as more than 100 years old, will enter duty-free despite functionality. The object must be accompanied by a statement from the seller or other person having competent knowledge of the facts indicating the place and approximate date of creation.

The rule for importing *ethnographic works* of art duty-free is that the item must be at least fifty years old. Much of the primitive art currently of interest to collectors was created more than fifty years ago and is, therefore, admitted duty-free under the ethnographic objects provision. More recent ethnographic works, however, are dutiable.

If work is considered to be a collector's item, it will enter duty-free. Collectors' items include such things as taxidermied animals, preserved insects and plants, fossils, archaeological material, minerals, human skeletal material and mummies, and coins and medals.

Works that are made from protected species may not enter the U.S. unless accompanied by an appropriate export license.

In order to protect U.S. copyrights and trademarks, Customs will seize any item that may be deemed to infringe registered U.S. copyrights, trademarks or patents. It is, therefore, essential for you to verify that the collectible you purchase abroad is not an infringing item. For example, it is quite common to find designer knock-offs, such as Rolex watches and Gucci bags, for exceptionally low prices. These knock-offs may not legally be imported into the United States, and you, as the importer, could be charged as an infringer. If the price on a patented, copyrighted or trademarked item seems to be too good to be true, it probably is—be cautious.

EFFECT OF FREE TRADE AGREEMENTS

The North American Free Trade Agreement (NAFTA) is eliminating tariffs between the United States, Canada and Mexico. About half of the tariffs were dropped in January 1994, with the remainder to be gradually phased out over time. This elimination of tariffs means that the duty barrier that would be in effect for works that do not qualify as art or antiquities, such as most crafts and non-qualifying prints, sculptures and other collectibles, will no longer exist for works imported from Canada and Mexico.

The European Union has phased out most tariffs, as well. The member countries as of the date of publication are Austria, Belgium, Denmark, Finland, France, Germany, Greece, Ireland, Italy, Luxembourg, The Netherlands, Portugal, Spain, Sweden and the United Kingdom. The expansion of the General Agreement on Tariffs and Trade (GATT) lowered tariffs an average of 33% on goods imported into member countries.

EXPORT RESTRICTIONS

Most nations have adopted laws to control the flow of certain cultural property across their borders in addition to customs duties and tariffs. These restrictions are necessary to help prevent looting and theft, as well as the export of national treasures and archaeological items.

Some countries use screening prohibitions, while others use across-the-board prohibitions. Screening prohibitions allow the country's government to decide whether a particular item should be allowed to be exported. Under the laws of Great Britain, for example, a license must be obtained to export any object more than 100 years old and valued at over £8,000 (sterling), which either was created in Britain or was imported into Britain at least fifty years prior to the date export is desired. The determination of whether to grant a license is made depending on the object's close connection with British history and national life, its aesthetic importance and its significance for academic study.

By contrast, complete prohibition systems ban the export of all pieces from a certain time, place or creator. A frequent consequence of this type of system is the escalation of black market operations. For example, Mexico has enacted such a law with respect to pre-Columbian art and, as a result, the market in illegally exported work from Mexico has flourished.

In countries with export restrictions, you often are required to obtain an export license in order to remove cultural property. Because this may take several months, it is frequently wisest for you to require the dealer from whom you purchase the work to apply for the license. You can also hire a customs agent to seek export approval.

Export restrictions are typically enforced by criminal sanctions or by provisions for forfeiture or both. Thus, it is important for you not only to adhere to export restrictions, but also to research the provenance of the works you contemplate purchasing. If it later turns out that a work was illegally exported, you may have to forfeit that work to its country of origin.

For example, criminal sanctions may be imposed by a country other than the work's country of origin. A U.S. federal district court held that defendants who conspired to obtain pre-Columbian artifacts in Guatemala and to sell them in the U.S. violated the U.S. National Stolen Property Act, which prohibits the transportation in interstate or foreign commerce of stolen goods worth $5,000 or more. The court's decision was based on its finding that Guatemalan law makes all pre-Columbian artifacts the property of the Guatemalan government. There was ample evidence to demonstrate that the defendants knew that Guatemalan law prohibited export of the artifacts.

IMPORT RESTRICTIONS

A few countries unilaterally refuse to admit art illegally exported from another country. There are also several bilateral treaties that prohibit the transport of certain categories of art and antiquities between the signatory nations.

Multilateral treaties accomplish many of the same objectives on a larger scale. Some are regional efforts, while others are more comprehensive. The UNESCO Convention on the Means of Prohibiting and Preventing the Illicit Import, Export and Transfer of Ownership of Cultural Property, for example, is a global effort.

The earliest signatory nations to the UNESCO Convention were primarily art-exporting countries such as Ecuador, Cameroon, Mexico, Egypt and Brazil, which caused some critics to doubt the effectiveness of the treaty. Since 1983, the United States has been a party to the Convention, making it an effective tool in controlling the illicit traffic in certain antiquities.

Under the UNESCO Convention, articles not accompanied by a certificate or other documentation from the country of origin certifying that the exportation was not illegal are subject to seizure and judicial forfeiture and must be offered for return to the country of origin. An article may be imported without a certificate if the importer furnishes satisfactory evidence that the article was exported from the country of origin ten years or more before the date of entry into the United States and that the importer acquired the article less than one year from the date of entry. Entry without a certificate also is allowed if the article was exported before it became protected.

ENDANGERED AND OTHER PROTECTED SPECIES

Many collectibles are created from materials that can be obtained only from endangered or other protected animal or botanical species. In an effort to save these creatures and plants from extinction, the international community, including the U.S., adopted a multilateral treaty called the Convention on International Trade in Endangered Species of Wild Fauna and Flora (CITES). The treaty regulates trade in certain protected materials, even when used in collectibles, by requiring member nations to regulate the issuance of export and import licenses. The process is not unlike issuing passports for animals to pass from country to country.

The United States has passed several laws intended to protect domestic endangered or threatened species and to bar the importation of items, including collectibles, containing parts from endangered or threatened species. Most of these statutes forbid the killing or trading of an endangered or otherwise protected species, whether or not the species is native to the U.S. These statutes are often stricter than required by CITES, and many states have enacted even more restrictive measures.

Be careful when buying items made using animal hides or bones, exotic woods, and the like.

If the species is endangered, you will likely have to forfeit the item. Criminal sanctions may be imposed, as well. When dealing, for example, with ivory, whale teeth, eagle feathers and parts, hawk and crow feathers and parts, trilliums, or the like, you must determine whether the acquisition or disposal is legally permitted. Check with museum curators or lawyers who specialize in the field. Laws such as the Eagle Protection Act and the Native American Graves Protection and Repatriation Act, among others, should be reviewed before the transaction occurs.

CHAPTER 13

<hr/>

When Your Artwork is Held by Others

Collectors should be aware of the legal relationship created when they transfer possession, but not ownership, of an item. This relationship arises when, for instance, you leave paintings with a framer for framing, or when you lend a collection to a museum or historical society for exhibition.

Bailment

Bailment is a legal term used to describe the situation where one is in rightful possession of another's property. A bailment can be for the benefit of the *bailor* (the property owner), of the *bailee* (the property holder), or both. In general, the standard of care imposed depends on the type of bailment. In a bailment for the benefit of the bailor, the bailee will be liable only for gross negligence. That is, the conduct complained of must be outrageous, including willful or intentional injuries, before the person in possession will be held responsible. In a bailment for the benefit of the bailee, the bailee will be liable for even slight negligence. This means that the person holding the work must be extraordinarily careful and will be responsible for even the slightest lapse in care and diligence. If the bailment benefits both parties—as where the bailee is paid for his or her services—ordinary care is required. In any event, a bailee must exercise reasonable care in protecting the item.

Bailments for Mutual Benefit

Collectors will most often engage in bailments for mutual benefit. Such bailments occur, for instance, when you pay a framing shop to frame a drawing, when you pay a base-maker to create a base for a sculpture, when you pay a conservator to clean a painting, when you pay a storage facility to store your doll collection, or when you pay an appraiser to appraise a work of glass art. In these situations, the bailee is required to exercise ordinary care.

As the bailee exercises ordinary care, he or she will not be liable even when your item is damaged, destroyed, lost or stolen while it was held by the bailee.

If, for example, your sculpture is stolen when the base-maker takes reasonable precautions against theft, the base-maker will not be liable. Similarly, if your drawing is destroyed by fire when the framer takes reasonable precautions to prevent fire, the framer will not be liable. This underscores the need for your insurance policy to cover artwork when it is off your premises.

Of course, if the appraiser negligently drops and destroys your work of glass art, if the storage facility negligently fails to provide proper security and your collection is stolen, or if the conservator negligently removes pigment while cleaning your painting, liability will be imposed. The careless bailee will have to pay for the damage done.

Frequently, the bailee will try to disclaim responsibility. You may be asked to sign a contract relieving the bailee of liability, or the receipt you are given when you turn over your work may contain a disclaimer. Generally, the language will say that the bailee is not liable for any loss of or damage. Such a disclaimer is usually enforceable, so long as your attention is drawn to it by the bailee or by its conspicuous appearance on the receipt or contract. These disclaimers will protect the bailee from liability for ordinary negligence, although you may still be able to recover for any intentional damage or gross negligence.

A bailment for mutual benefit also occurs where you hire a ship-ping company to transport your collection. In this situation, however, the standard of care is increased. With few exceptions, a common car-rier is liable for any loss of or damage to property in its custody. A com-mon carrier is any business that publicly offers to transport goods for a fee, including truck companies, bus lines, railroads and airlines. The company may, however, limit its liability if it provides greater coverage for an increased fee. You should determine whether the insurance you have on items in your collection will be in effect while the pieces are in transit. If your insurance does have this form of coverage, then you may not need to purchase additional insur-ance from a carrier. If your collection is insured only while on your premises, then purchasing additional coverage for items in transit is appropriate. Federal regulations limit liability for loss, damage or destruction to items in the possession of common carriers.

This underscores the importance of either purchasing extra insurance when transporting items, or verify-ing that your existing insurance covers your items while they are in transit on a common carrier.

LOANS

Collectors often lend artworks, antiques, or whole collections to muse-ums or other institutions, such as libraries, historical societies, or schools. Lending of collectibles may not only reduce maintenance costs to the owner, but may also enhance your reputation and boost the value of your collection. Further benefits may include the services of an institution's conservators and researchers. You should, however, be aware of the risks of loaning your collectibles, and take steps to mini-mize these risks.

When you lend a collectible to an institution for exhibition, a bail-ment for the benefit of the bailee is created. This means that the insti-tution will be liable for even slight negligence. So long as the institution exercises extreme care in dealing with your property, however, the institution will not be responsible for damage to or loss of your item. Because of the possibility that your work may, for instance, be stolen or destroyed by fire through no fault of the institution, you will probably want to require the institution to insure your collectible. This can be provided for in the loan agreement.

A loan agreement should always be in writing and signed by both you and an authorized representative of the institution. This agreement should contain the name and address of the lender and the borrower, a detailed description and value of the item(s), the duration of the loan, and the other terms and conditions of the loan, including an identification of who is responsible for insuring the work both during the term of the loan and while in transit.

The institution generally will agree to insure the item(s). This insurance should be a *wall-to-wall* policy covering the work from the moment it leaves your premises until the moment it returns. The value of the work, and thus, the amount of coverage, should also be specified in the agreement. Because most loan agreements require the collector to agree to accept the amount paid by the insurance company as full compensation for any loss, you should be sure the coverage is adequate. If, during the period of the loan, the value of the work increases, you should amend the loan agreement and request an increase in the coverage.

Some collectors choose to insure loaned works under their own policies because they believe their coverage is superior, or because they prefer to deal with their own insurance company in the event of a claim. If you prefer to insure a work under your own policy, you can request that the institution reimburse you for the premium. If the institution agrees to reimbursement, it generally will require you to either add the institution as an additional insured or to provide a waiver of subrogation against it, which means that your insurance company will not sue the institution for reimbursement in the event of a claim. Most loan agreements provide that, unless otherwise specified in the document, you release the institution from any liability in connection with the loan.

Providing that you own them, the work is functional, or the creator's rights have lapsed, reproduction rights also may be granted in the loan agreement, since the institution may wish to photograph the work for its catalog, publicity and/or educational purposes. If you own the copyright in the work, you should require the institution to protect your copyright. If you do not own the copyright or the right to reproduce the work and the work is not functional or in the public domain, you may not grant reproduction rights, and the loan agreement should reflect this fact.

A loan agreement should also identify the party responsible for the cost of crating and shipping the work, and when and how notice is to be given if ownership of the work changes during the period of the loan.

Before lending any work, you should assess its condition. Be sure that it can withstand the strains of packing, shipping and display. If you determine that the work is travel worthy, you should describe the work's condition in writing and take photographs as verification. Send a copy of the document and photographs to the borrowing institution. You also may wish to have the borrower prepare a written *condition report* when the work arrives and another just before it is returned. Be certain that the borrowing institution is capable of caring for the work properly. Ask about building construction, security, fire protection, climate control and lighting.

The mere fact that your work is being loaned to an institution does not necessarily mean that the institution has modern fire and theft protection, conservation, or the like. Regrettably, some cultural institutions fall short of adhering to state-of-the-art practices.

> *It is important for you to independently evaluate the merits of a borrower and the benefits you may derive from lending items in your collection.*

Prudence, attention to detail and common sense should be an important part of the evaluation and implementation of any loan arrangement.

Some collectors feel that identifying themselves as the owner of important works, whether in the media or while on loan, is an invitation to be burglarized. It is for this reason that many loans are identified as *anonymous*. Some lenders will permit the use of their name only in connection with loans that are made to institutions outside of their home state. You should determine whether the notoriety you will receive from being publicly identified as the owner of certain works is desirable for you, in light of the additional attention you may attract from some undesirable sources.

The law of bailment is quite technical and, before agreeing to commit work from your collection, you should consult an experienced business lawyer and determine whether the proposed arrangement is acceptable. The mere fact that an institution is involved or that it has printed forms does not necessarily mean that the terms are non-negotiable. An experienced attorney should be able to identify potential problems and bring them to your attention. For more information related to loans of art and artifacts, see

http://arts.endow.gov/guide/Indemnity/Intro.html

Glossary

A

absentee bidding. The process by which someone not attending an auction is permitted to bid on an item at that auction. Customarily, this is required by an *auction house* to be in a writing identifying the item and the maximum price that the bidder will offer for the item. A representative of the *auction house* then bids at the auction on behalf of the absentee bidder up to the authorized absentee-bid amount. Experienced *auctioneers* will rarely, if ever, call attention to the fact that there is an absentee bid being made.

actual damages. The amount of damages actually suffered and that can be proven regarding a loss. If a painting valued at $100,000 is destroyed the actual damage is $100,000.

antiquities. A work of art, piece of furniture, or collectible made or created at a notable time in the past, customarily at least over 100 years ago.

appraisal. The process of having an item valued. The appraiser's credentials, as well as the method used to establish the value, are important in determining the credibility of the appraisal. Appraisals are generally written and are frequently required when items are, for example, donated to charity for purposes of obtaining a tax deduction, obtaining insurance, or recovery when an insured loss occurs.

appraised value. The value or worth that an item is determined to have by an appraiser. The actual market value or selling price may be higher or lower than the appraised value, but the *appraisal* may be used for purposes of obtaining insurance or for making a charitable donation. Frequently, an appraiser's opinion must be in writing and specify the appraiser's credentials so that recipients of the appraisal will be able to evaluate its credibility.

as is. A term customarily used in sales of items that were previously owned. The *Uniform Commercial Code* makes it clear that, when selling used items, words such as "as is," "with all faults," or the like are intended to put prospective purchasers on notice of the fact that there are no *warranties*, expressed or implied, with respect to the item being sold.

ascending-bid method. *See English method.*

auction catalog. This catalog is prepared before an auction for purposes of identifying the items to be auctioned and providing the auction house with an opportunity to describe the items in some detail. These catalogs are generally made available for purchase at a pre-auction viewing of the items to be sold. Many auction houses have subscribers who receive auction catalogs by mail so that the recipients may bid by either *absentee bid* or telephone bid on items they wish to acquire. Subscribers to auction catalogs frequently receive *post-sale sheets* for purposes of determining the prices actually paid for items in an auction. Catalogs and *post-sale prices* may also be available online. *See also presale catalog.*

auction house. The place where an *auction* is conducted. This term is sometimes used to refer to the business which conducts the auction as well; for instance, Sotheby Parke Bernet and Christie's might be considered auction houses. Online auction sites, such as eBay and Yahoo!, may also be considered to be auction houses.

auction. The process of selling items through competitive bidding. An auction may include bidding on works that are owned by the *auction house* or *consigned* to it.

auctioneer. The person who conducts an *auction*. The auctioneer does not hold legal title to the item but, rather, acts as a selling agent for that item. Auctioneers are generally licensed by the state in which they practice. There are a number of schools throughout the world that specialize in training individuals to become auctioneers; one of the most famous is the London-based Sotheby Parke Bernet Auction School.

authenticity. The quality or state of being authentic. An item that is authentic is an item that is what it is purported to be. In the case of artwork that is attributed to a particular artist, an authentic work would be work actually by that artist and not by a forger. In the case of antiquities, an authentic item would be one which is actually of the age, quality, and material that it is described to be.

autoradiography. The process of producing an image on a photographic film or plate using radiation from a radioactive substance.

B

bailee. A legal term used to define one who is in rightful possession of another's work. A bailee does not have legal *title* to the work, merely the right to possess it. A museum, for example, displaying the works of others for a particular exhibition, would be considered a bailee of these works.

bailment. The process by which work is transferred to a *bailee* for purposes of fulfilling the arrangement.

bailor. The person or entity providing another with possession of an item for some lawful purpose. Customarily, the bailor is the legal owner of the item.

bid confirmation form. Written documentation signed by the successful bidder at an auction to bind the sale.

bidding off the chandelier. *See phantom bid.*

bid—in. The process whereby, in an auction with *reserve*, the bids do not equal or exceed the reserve. In this event, the item will not be sold, and it is said that the *auction house* or owner has bid—in. *Post-sale sheets* will state that the item was either bid—in or that the *reserve price* had not been met, or words to that effect.

bill of sale. A form, usually signed by the seller or the seller's representative, confirming a sale. It should, among other things, describe with some particularity the item sold, the price paid, the identity of the purchaser, and any other relevant information surrounding the sale. Some states require documentation when limited-edition works, such as prints or sculptures, are sold. This disclosure may be contained in the bill of sale. A bill of sale does not necessarily transfer *legal title*; rather, it merely confirms the terms of the arrangement. *See also editioned work and legal title.*

bona fide purchaser. One who acquires an item without knowledge of any legal problem with respect to the seller's ownership; an example of a legal problem would be an item consigned to a *dealer* through a fraudulent action. This should be distinguished from a situation where stolen items are involved; no one can acquire good *title* from a thief, and the legitimate owner can always reclaim a stolen piece, even if acquired by a bona fide purchaser.

branded as burned. A slang term referring to an item which has been discredited and is identified as such. Frequently, this refers to a work that is classified as a fake or forgery. In *auctions*, this refers to an item that did not sell either because there were no bids or the *reserve price* was not met.

bronze disease. Occurs when chloride and oxygen combine in a damp environment, causing the bronze to deteriorate. It is evidenced by rough, light green spots that appear on the work and result in its ultimate deterioration. Bronze disease can also attack brass and pewter.

business liquidation. The process whereby a business is closed down. All of the assets, including not only the merchandise but also the fixtures, are sold, and the business ultimately ceases to exist.

buy now. A term used in *online auctions* where a bidder can end the auction by agreeing to pay a set price.

buyer's premium. *Auction* participants may be required to pay this premium when they participate in an auction; thus, a buyer's premium of 10% means that a bid accepted for $1,000 will be subject to a buyer's premium of $100. The successful purchaser will, therefore, actually pay

$1,100, rather than the $1,000 bid at the auction. Note that the successful bidder may also have to pay any applicable sales tax as well. Not all *auction houses* impose buyer's premiums.

C

capital asset. An asset other than inventory.

catalog. *See auction catalog and presale catalog.*

certificate of authenticity. A certificate that states that the item is what it is represented to be. Thus, if a work of art is described as having been created by a particular artist, then the certificate of authenticity would be a written representation of the fact that the work is by that particular artist. If the item is an antiquity, then the certificate would represent that the item is of the age and possessing the qualities represented. A certificate of authenticity is a written *express warranty* with respect to the items covered by it. Many contemporary collectibles are accompanied by certificates of authenticity describing characteristics of the items, such as precious metal content, maker's name, period of creation or the like. Many of these are intended to establish some means of officially enhancing the value by some restrictive criteria. *See also authenticity and editioned works.*

certification marks. Marks that are used to certify specific characteristics of works. Frequently, these marks are registered with the U.S. Trademark Office and are protected under the federal statute. Certification marks may be used, for example, to certify that work is created by a Native American group, made in Alaska, or that the work has passed certain quality tests, such as those given by Underwriters Lab. *See also hallmark.*

chargeback. The process whereby credit card companies may force merchants to return money received when the credit card charge is challenged by the credit card owner.

coinsurance. A provision in an insurance policy whereby the *insured* is permitted to obtain insurance equal to a specific percentage, usually 80% or more, of the value of the item insured. If there is a loss, then the insured may recover the total value of the loss up to the face amount of the policy. If, on the other hand, the insured obtains insurance for less than the specified percentage of the value of the item insured, then the insurance company takes the position that it is essentially sharing in the cost of insurance, and, as a result, it should be permitted to share in the loss. The amount of recovery is, thus, pro rated. For example, if a work of art worth $100,000 is partially damaged in a covered claim, such as a fire loss, and the insurance carried on the work was only $50,000, then the insurance company will consider itself a partner. In this event, the work valued at $100,000 and insured for one-half of its value will entitle the insured to obtain a recovery equal to one-half of the loss sustained. Thus, if it would cost $25,000 to repair the work, the insured would be entitled to recover only $12,500, since the insurance company would take the position that it was a 50% partner in the insurance and entitled to retain 50% of the value of the loss. Also referred to as *coinsurance clause*.

commission. The amount paid for either work performed or services rendered. For instance, an art *dealer* would generally receive a commission for selling artwork for someone else.

commissioning. The process by which an arrangement is made to perform a particular lawful act. When one *commissions* an artist to paint a portrait, the artist is being hired for the purpose of painting the portrait, and the arrangement is referred to as commissioning.

comparative analysis. A technique to authenticate an item where the compounds making up a work, such as a particular type of color of paint, are dated and compared to know substance used at that time.

compilations. An original copyrightable work that is created by collecting and arranging literary works in an original way. The arrangement of the works makes it original, not the pre-existing works themselves.

confederate. One who works with another to create an unsavory arrangement. For example, in an arrangement between prospective purchasers at an *auction* where one purchaser discredits a piece while the other bids on it, or where purchasers inhibit a legitimate auction by agreeing not to bid against one another, the individuals in such arrangements may be referred to as confederates.

conservation. The process of preserving art and antiquities, including, among other things, cleaning and preservation.

conservator. A person who specializes in cleaning and preserving works of art or antiquities.

consignment. An arrangement whereby work is entrusted to a person or entity for purposes of sale. The one who holds the work is referred to as the consignee, and the consignee does not obtain legal title to the work. Rather, the consignee is permitted to display and transfer the work to a purchaser. If the item is not sold, then, in accordance with the consignment arrangement, the work generally is returned to the owner who provided it initially, referred to as the *consignor*.

consignor. A person, generally the artist or owner of a work, who gives the right to sell his or her work to others.

copyright. The right to make copies. Generally the rights granted and governed by the Copyright Revision Act of 1976. Copyright encompasses five exclusive rights—the right to reproduce a work by any means; the right to prepare derivative works based on the copyrighted work; the right to distribute copies to the public for sale or lease; the right to perform a work publicly where appropriate; and, the right to display the work publicly. Copyright protection is granted to "original works of authorship fixed in any tangible medium of expression."

customs. Duties, tolls or taxes imposed by a government on transactions across its borders.

D

dealer. An art dealer is generally one who buys, sells and otherwise deals in art. In the *Uniform Commercial Code*, a dealer is defined as a merchant for purposes of that body of law.

decedent. A legal term describing someone who has died.

depreciation. The decline in value of an item. For tax purposes, the amount an item loses in value over time.

derivative work. A work based on a pre-existing piece that only the owner of the original piece has the right to produce or grant permission to another to avoid a copyright infringement claim.

descending-bid method. *See Dutch method.*

disclosed bidding. A classic form of bidding where participants in an auction are identified and bid by either raising a bidding paddle or in some other way making it clear that they are actually participating in the auction.

droit de suite. The French term describing the resale royalties rights an artist retains even after a work is sold. Recognized widely in Europe, but only limitedly in the U.S.

droit moral. The French term for the rights attached to a piece of work that stay with the creator even after the piece is sold. *See also moral rights.*

dutch method. A type of *auction* whereby the item is identified, and the *auctioneer* presents a price that is likely to be higher than that at which the item would sell. The auctioneer then reduces the price in stages until an auction participant acknowledges that the price stated is acceptable. The first participant to agree to a stated price is the party to whom the item will be sold. Dutch auctions may be conducted in person by an actual *auctioneer* or through an online or written procedure. In such situations, the business presenting the auction displays the price online or by a posting, and the price is periodically reduced until a participant agrees to acquire the item for the designated price. Also referred to as *descending-bid method.*

E

eBay. An online auction house where numerous collectibles and other fine art pieces are available.

editioned work. Work that is reproduced in the form of prints, posters, collectibles or a series of sculptures. Editioned work can either be limited or unlimited. A limited-edition work requires the work to be limited to the number stated, and many jurisdictions have passed laws requiring disclosure of certain facts with respect to limited-edition works. These disclosures are often in the form of certificates, which become *express warranties* regarding the number of pieces in the edition and other characteristics. Editioned works can be produced by hand, through the hand-printing process or hand-casting of sculptures, or by a photo, mechanical, or other automated process. A buyer of an editioned work should request a *certificate of authenticity* specifying the number of pieces in the edition, the method by which it was created, whether the artist is alive or stating that the work is posthumous, and any other characteristics deemed important with respect to the item in question. *See also bill of sale and certificate of authenticity.*

English method. Customarily, the *auctioneer* in a traditional *auction* solicits bids or offers from the participants, and accepts the highest bid or offer in order to consummate the sale. The method by which the highest bid or offer is accepted varies from auction to auction, but would traditionally include statements such as "going, going, gone" and "sold," or by slamming down a hammer or mallet. Also referred to as *ascending-bid method*, or *traditional auction.*

escrow agent. An independent third party who has possession of an item and/or money in an *escrow* arrangement.

escrow. An arrangement whereby a third person who is independent of either the buyer or seller holds either the item to be sold, the purchase price, or both, with clear instructions regarding the terms of the transaction. Such terms include: the conditions upon which the work is to be transferred to the buyer; the manner upon which the buyer is allowed access to the work for examination; the circumstances upon which the work is returned to the seller; as well as the conditions upon which the purchase price is to be paid to the seller or returned to the buyer. This arrangement is similar to that used in many states for the purchase and sale of real estate, as well as other items of value, such as art and antiques.

escrow agent. The person independent of either the buyer or seller who holds the work or purchase price in escrow.

estate. The personal property and obligations left by a person at death.

estate sale. A term traditionally describing the sale of a person's possessions after that person's death. Historically, an estate sale has been used to liquidate the assets of a deceased person in order to pay funeral and other expenses necessary to wind down an estate or comply with the descendant's wishes or the law. Use of the term has evolved and, today, it is used to describe other forms of sales as well. It includes, for example, sales of household and other goods when persons are retiring, downsizing a household, or moving. There are businesses that specialize in conducting estate sales and assist with pricing, cataloging, and conducting the sales.

ethnographic works. Works that are produced by a certain ethnic group or in a certain geographical location. Generally described as primitive art.

exclusivity contract. A contract whereby a party is given the exclusive right to participate in a specific arrangement. In this situation, no other person may have the right that is the subject of the particular contract, and, when the arrangement is for purposes of sale, even the owner (as distinguished from the person granted the exclusive right to sell) may not engage in selling the item. If a *dealer* is granted the exclusive right to sell a work, then that dealer has an exclusivity contract, and is the only one who may conduct the sale.

export. The act of shipping something to another country.

express warranty. A *warranty* that is expressed either in writing or orally.

F

fair comment defense. A defense to either defamation of a person or product disparagement (when an item is being disparaged). The fact that a comment is defended as a "fair comment" does not necessarily mean that it is true but, rather, that the speaker is constitutionally permitted (under the First Amendment of the U.S. Constitution) to express that opinion.

fair use. A defense used in the area of copyright law where someone's use of copyrighted material is excused though unauthorized. To be a fair use the use must be reasonable and limited. Putting a picture of a copyrighted piece up for sale in a in an auction catalog is probably a fair use of that piece.

fine art. Includes paintings, sculptures, drawings, architecture, poetry, music, dance, and dramatic arts. It should be distinguished from commercial art, such as that which appears in advertising. It should also be distinguished from functional items, which may be ornamental and beautiful but do not rise to the level of being characterized as fine art.

first sale doctrine. A rule in copyright law that once the copyright owner (usually the creator) sells the piece, he or she losses the right to interfere with later sales of the same work.

fixed price. The stated or posted price of an item.

free bidding. A manner of bidding in the English method where the bidders make bids on their own accord.

G

good title. *See title.*

guaranteed price. An amount an auction house guarantees it will sell a piece for at auction.

generalized system of preference (GSP). A customs law enacted to provide certain underdeveloped countries with the ability to have some of their commodities enter the U.S. without tariffs.

H

hallmark. An artisan's mark, customarily found on works of metal, china, porcelain or the like, that provides information about the creation of the work. The marks may identify the artist or studio, the date of creation, the material used and the like. Historically, hallmarks were used to identify the craft guild to which the creator belonged and the actual creator. In this way, the purchaser of a work would be able to trace it if there were a defect in workmanship, material or the like. Today, these marks are used to verify *authenticity*, though many forgeries exist.

hammer price. The price for which a work is sold at auction. Note that this does not include either the *buyer's premium* or sales tax. Also referred to as *knockdown*.

I

identification marks. Marks on items used to identify them. In the case of bronze casting, frequently foundries and artists identify their works by using identification marks. In addition, museums and important collectors frequently mark their works for purposes of future identification. *See also hallmark.*

implied warranty. A form of *warranty* that is implied by law and attaches to every sale specified by the law. For example, the *Uniform Commercial Code* provides that in every sale of goods, there is implied a warranty that the item will be merchantable, and, if the seller knows the buyer's purpose for purchasing the item, then the item must be fit for that purpose. These warranties (*warranty of merchantability* and *warranty of fitness* for a particular purpose) may be eliminated, and the statute provides specific methods by which they can be disclaimed. *See also warranty of title and warranty of noninfringement.*

import. The act of shipping something into a country.

independent contractor. One who provides a service for another but who is not an employee of that other. An independent contractor conducts his or her own business and enjoys the status of an independent business for purposes of local, state and federal employment laws (including taxes).

in-painting. The process of filling in spaces on a painting which have occurred as a result of age or other deterioration. This is a type of *restoration* and should be performed by a very skilled restorer.

insured. The person for whose benefit insurance is obtained.

intermediary. A person or institution acting as an agent or other facilitator between a buyer and seller.

J

Japanese method. A type of *auction* whereby the *auctioneer* permits participants to simultaneously present bids through the use of hand signals, confidential written submissions, or the like. The auctioneer will accept the bid desired from the simultaneous submissions and, customarily, will accept the highest price offered. This method of conducting an auction is frequently used in the West by governments that put construction contracts out to bid. In such situations, the job is described, qualified applicants are provided with an opportunity to ask questions related to the job, and the applicants are then provided a period within which to submit a sealed bid. The bids must be submitted on or before the time and date specified, and the municipality requesting the bids reviews the proposals and announces the identity of the successful bidder. This process is seldom used for the sale of art and antiques in the West. Also referred to as *simultaneous method.*

joint buying. Where two or more individuals join together as one to make purchases at an *auction.*

M

microscopic techniques. A scientific method of authenticating a piece using microscopic analysis.

moral rights. Rights artists retain in their artwork even after it is sold. These rights are more generally recognized in Europe, but are, to a varying degree, recognized in parts of the United States. These rights include: the right to create or to refrain from creating, allowing the artist to be the sole judge of whether his or her work is ready to be displayed; the right to disclosure, which allows an artist or craftsperson to prevent someone else from publishing a work that the creative person has discarded; the right to withdraw a work after it has been disclosed (not recognized in the United States); the right to prevent the use of the artist's name as the creator of the work if the work has been distorted, mutilated, or otherwise modified so as to injure the artist's honor or reputation; the right to prevent the destruction of a work of recognized stature; and the right to be protected from excessive criticism.

Multiples. *See editioned works.*

N

nail-to-nail. An insurance term for coverage provided when items are insured in one location, transferred to another location, and returned to the original location. The term's origin comes from the fact that a painting is hung on a nail in one's home, rehung on a nail within a museum, for example, and then returned to the original nail in one's home. The term is also used to describe such coverage for sculptures and antiquities, even though they are not displayed on nails.

O

online auctions. *Auctions* that are conducted on the World Wide Web. The most famous of these is *eBay*, and the process is similar to a live auction, although it takes longer. Items to be sold are described and depicted on the website. The *auction house* establishes rules for sales, including items which may be sold. For example, *eBay* does not permit sale of Nazi memorabilia, artifacts from the Shuttle Columbia disaster, or human beings or body parts. Rules for sales are posted on the *auction house's* site. Bidders who qualify based on the *auction house's* guidelines are permitted to post their offers for items. An offer for an item remains open for a fixed period of time, during which time the bidding continues. If the auction is *with reserve* and the *reserve price* has been met or exceeded, then the person who meets or exceeds the reserve and offers the highest price for the item within the permitted time will be permitted to purchase the item. The online auction house will frequently establish the arrangement whereby the item to be sold and the purchase price for that item are exchanged. *See also escrow.*

ordinary purpose. A term used with warranties that refers to the normal and customary use of a particular thing.

outright purchase. The acquisition of an item for value. The term is customarily used to describe the arrangement whereby a gallery, *dealer*, or the like acquires legal *title* to a work by buying it, rather than having that work merely *consigned* to it for purposes of resale.

overvaluation. For tax purposes, overvaluation occurs when a claimed value for a piece exceeds its actual value. The IRS will impose penalties if claiming, for example, a charitable deduction for a donated piece, and the deducted amount is greater than what the piece is actually worth.

over-insurance. If a policy is taken out for an amount that exceeds the value of the item insured, then it is said to be over-insured, and, even if there is a total loss of the over-insured item, no more than the actual value of the insured item may be recovered.

owner's agent. A person acting on behalf of and for an owner of a piece of art or other collectible.

P

particular purpose. A term used with warranties that refers to the specific knowledge a seller must have in regards to what the buyer intends to do with the item being purchased. What the buyer intends to do with an item may not be what it is originally used for.

patina. The surface coating of an item. This term frequently refers to the appearance of a bronze which results from treatment by salts, acids, or the like.

phantom bid. As the term suggests, a phantom bid is not an actual bid. It occurs when an *auctioneer* improperly (and in some jurisdictions, unlawfully) suggests that a bid is being offered when, in fact, no such bid has been made. The process, known as *running the bidding*, is used by unethical auctioneers for the purpose of artificially increasing the price bid for an item. Under the *Uniform Commercial Code*, a purchaser who learns that phantom bidding has been employed may return the item purchased or purchase the item for the last good-faith bid actually made. In order to avoid being trapped by phantom bidding, experienced *auction* participants sit as far back in the auction house as possible so that they can actually see their competition.

post-sale prices. The prices for which the items at an *auction* were actually sold. These are frequently posted on the Web, and a *post-sale sheet* containing them may be provided to subscribers of *auction catalogs*.

post-sale sheet. A physical sheet or sheets containing the actual prices for which items were sold at an *auction*; generally available to those who subscribe to an *auction catalog* in advance of an auction and receive the post-sale sheet containing the actual prices of the works after the auction has been completed. *See also post-sale prices.*

premium. The price paid by a policyholder to an insurance company for insurance.

presale catalog. A catalog prepared before a sale. This is commonly used by *auction houses* for purposes of providing attendees with an opportunity to learn the character of the *auction* and to provide the auction house's description of the items being auctioned. Many auction houses sell subscriptions to their presale catalogs. Some post their *catalog* and *post-sale sheets* on the World Wide Web, eliminating the need to subscribe for these items. Either *absentee bidding* or telephone bidding is sometimes used to participate in an auction from remote locations.

presumption of consignment. A legal term that implies that a piece delivered by an artist to a dealer for sale is to do so on consignment.

provenance. The lineage or history of ownership of the work in question. Works may have enhanced value by virtue of a provenance; thus, a work that was previously owned by a museum will likely, as a result of that fact alone, have more market appeal than one that has never been owned by anyone famous or important in the art world.

pseudonymity. The use of a fictitious name.

public domain. Works which are not protected by copyright law, usually because the copyright protection has expired, are said to be in the public domain. Works in the public domain can be used, reproduced or otherwise copied by anyone without liability for copyright infringement.

R

radiocarbon dating. A scientific method of authenticating a piece that determines the age of an item by measuring the amount of carbon 14 it contains.

ransom insurance. Insurance purchased to cover stolen art work that is being ransomed back to the true owner.

recast. *See restrike.*

reproductions. *See multiples and editioned works.*

resale royalty. The right an artist retains in a sold work to receive future commissions if a buyer sells the piece to another.

rescind the purchase. To cancel a purchase and return the work for a refund of your purchase price.

reserve amount. *See reserve price.*

reserve price. In the United States, most *auctions* are conducted *with reserve* or subject to a reserve price. This is an arrangement whereby the owner of the item to be auctioned establishes a minimum acceptable price which must be bid before the item may be sold. It is customarily not disclosed at the auction, and, unless the bids equal or exceed the reserve price, the item will be returned to the owner and not sold (this is referred to as being *bid—in*). Once the reserve price is met, then the item will be sold to the highest bidder. If an auction is held *without reserve*, then it is frequently advertised as such, since this means that the item will be sold to the highest bidder regardless of how low the highest offer is.

restoration. The process whereby an item, generally a work of art or antiquity, is restored to its original state after it has deteriorated from age or disaster. A classic example of a famous restoration is the process by which the Sistine Chapel ceiling was cleaned and restored to what is believed to be its appearance when it was completed by Michelangelo.

restrike. A process of creating a mold from an existing bronze and casting a new work from that mold. The work thus created is referred to as a restrike or recast.

rider. An amendment to an insurance policy which adds coverage or items insured. Thus, a standard homeowners policy might have a rider for purposes of adding coverage for identified artwork, jewelry, antiquities, or the like.

ring of buyers. A group of buyers at auction who have joined together in secret agreement not to compete against each other to control the prices at which a piece sells.

running the bid. *See phantom bid.*

S

schedule. A list of items insured. The list would customarily include both a description of the piece of artwork or the antiquity, and the value or appraisal of the item.

scientific authentication. A scientific process whereby the work, by virtue of certain scientific tests, is identified as being of the age, material, or substance that the test(s) establishes. Scientific authentication may not be used for purposes of identifying the work as having been created by a particular artist, since there is no scientific test available at this time that can establish that fact. Scientific authentication is more objective than stylistic authentication and is based on scientific data.

simultaneous method. *See Japanese method.*

statutory damages.   Damages that are described by, with an amount usually set, by a specific statutory law. An amount predetermined and/or capped by a legislative body.

stylistic authentication.   The form of authentication whereby an expert is able to identify a work based on its style. This is not a precise science, since the expert must use experience, know-how, intuition, and other investigative techniques in order to determine whether the style of the work in question is more likely than not to be the style of a particular artist. When the evaluation is not clear cut, the expert may characterize the work as "in the manner of an artist" or "based on the style of artist" or "from the school of an artist." These terms make it clear that the work is likely not by the identified artist but, rather, is similar to that person's work. Stylistic authentication is subjective.

T

tax value.   The value attributed to a work for tax purposes. Works of art are appraised for tax purposes in at least two situations: first, when an item is donated to a charity and the donor wishes to take a tax deduction for the donation; and second, when an item is valued for purposes of determining the size of an estate after the death of its owner. In both situations, it is important to obtain a written *appraisal* from a qualified appraiser. Generally, the donor of a work to a charity will hope for a high appraisal while the representative of an estate will prefer a low appraisal.

thermoluminescent analysis (TL). A scientific method of authenticating a piece and used to date ceramic goods.

title. Refers to ownership of an item and implies that the person who has this status enjoys rightful possession of the item as against everyone in the world. That person is characterized as the actual or true owner of the item in question. Also referred to as *legal title*.

trademark. A word, phrase, symbol, or logo that identifies ownership of an item the mark is attached to, and legally reserves the exclusive use of that mark to the owner.

trusts. A distinct legal entity often used in estate planing to transfer property, avoid probate, and minimize taxes.

U

underinsurance. A situation where the insurance purchased is less than the value of the item insured. If *coinsurance* is involved, the policy permits an insured to purchase a specified percentage of the value of the item insured and still recover the full amount of the loss up to the face value of the policy. (Compare to *over-insurance*.)

undisclosed bidding: A form of bidding describing a process of participating in an *auction* in a covert manner. Undisclosed bidders may arrange with an *auctioneer* to use some form of signal for the purpose of either entering a bid, or, if it is agreed that the individual will participate until otherwise designated, ceasing to bid. This form of bidding may be used by *dealers* or others who fear that their participation in an auction may, in and of itself, cause offers to increase. Famous people who wish to bid at auctions frequently do so through undisclosed agents or *absentee* or telephone bids, or occasionally through undisclosed bidding.

Uniform Commercial Code (UCC). A body of commercial law enacted in every state of the union, covering all forms of commercial transactions. The UCC deals with securities, commercial paper, vehicles, artwork, and the like. The Uniform Commission on State Laws periodically reviews this body of law and proposes updates, which must be considered by each state and, if acceptable, adopted as amendments to the existing body of commercial law.

unvalued policy. *See valued policy.*

V

valued policy. Insurance purchased for art and antiques, generally is referred to as a "floater" policy which can either be valued or unvalued. With a valued policy, the value of the item is established when the policy is first obtained, and any loss is paid at that amount. With an unvalued policy, the item will be valued at the time of the loss, and the insurance will pay the actual value of the item up to the face amount of the policy.

W

wall-to-wall. An insurance term referring to the scope of coverage for a particular location. It would include, for example, all of the items within an identified gallery, residence, or the like.

warranty. A contract, agreement or form of guaranty. *See also express warranty and implied warranty.*

warranty of authenticity. A *warranty* given by the seller or dealer that states the work being purchased is what it is represented to be. It is given when a *certificate of authenticity* from the creator is not available.

warranty of fitness for a particular purpose. If the seller knows of the buyer's purpose for acquiring an item, then there may be a *warranty* that that item will be fit for that purpose. This warranty may be expressed either in writing or through oral statements, and, pursuant to the Uniform Commercial Code, is implied in every transaction involving art and antiques. *See also implied warranty.*

warranty of merchantability. A *warranty* whereby the item is guarantied as merchantable; that is, the item would pass without objection in the trade under the description for that item. If a sample or model is used, there is a warranty that a merchantable item will conform to the model. *See also implied warranty.*

warranty of noninfringement. A *warranty* or guaranty that the work in question does not infringe or invade the rights of another. Typically, this warranty would be implied in the sale of any work of art, and, if it turns out that the item is an infringing work, the purchaser may insist upon having the seller assume responsibility for defending any infringement litigation. *See also implied warranty.*

warranty of title. A *warranty* whereby the seller guaranties that the seller has good title to the item in question and the right to convey that item. This warranty may be expressed in writing or orally, or, under the *Uniform Commercial Code* implied by virtue of the transaction. *See also implied warranty.*

with reserve. *See reserve price.*

without reserve. *See reserve price.*

work-for-hire. Under copyright law, a work produced by an employee of another, or independent contractor, for the employer or commissioning person in which the employer owns the copyright, not the actual producer.

X

x-ray detraction. A scientific method of authenticating a work used to discover material composition.

APPENDIX A

List of Organizations

The organizations listed below may be useful when dealing with art, antiquities, and other collectibles. No list such as this can be complete and comprehensive. Consult your local Yellow Pages, the World Wide Web, and local museums and other institutions involved with art, antiquities, and other collectibles for additional recommendations.

NOTE: *Since the Web is in constant flux and websites are appearing and disappearing with some frequency, no list such as this can be complete, accurate, and up-to-date. The reader is, therefore, urged to independently verify all addresses, phone numbers and, where possible, indices for more current information.*

American Craft Council
72 Spring Street
New York, NY 10012
212-274-0630
212-274-0650 (fax)
www.craftcouncil.org
membership@craftcouncil.org

The American Institute for Conservation of Historic and Artistic Works (AIC)
1717 K Street NW, Suite 200
Washington, DC 20006
202-452-9545
202-452-9328 (fax)
http://aic.stanford.edu
info@aic-faic.org

American Numismatic Association
(coin collecting)
818 North Cascade Avenue
Colorado Springs, CO 80903
www.money.org

American Philatelic Society
(stamp collecting)
www.west.net/~stamps1/aps.html

The American Society of Appraisers
555 Herndon Parkway, Suite 125
Herndon, VA 20170
703-478-2228
703-742-8471 (fax)
www.appraisers.org
asainfo@appraisers.org

Antiques and Fine Art
125 Walnut Street
Watertown, MA 047
www.antiquesandfineart.com
(Website has a locator site for
many forms of art, antiquities and
collectibles, and a dealer locator and
antique and art locator by type, origin or era, and a calender of featured
shows and events.)

The Appraisers Association of America
386 Park Avenue South, Suite 2000
New York, NY 10016
212-889 5404
212-889 5503 (fax)
www.appraisersassoc.org
aaa1@rcn.com

The Art Dealers Association of America, Inc. (ADAA)
575 Madison Avenue
New York, NY 10022
212-940-8590
212-940 6484 (fax)
www.artdealers.org
adaa@artdealers.org

The Association of International Photography Art Dealers, Inc.
1609 Connecticut Avenue, N.W.
Washington, DC 20009
202-986-0105
202-986-0448 (fax)
www.artline.com/associations/ipa
  /ipa.html
aipad@aol.com

Christie's
(international auction house)
20 Rockefeller Plaza
New York, NY 10020
212 636 2000
www.christies.com
info@christies.com

Collectimatica
100 Butte Loop
Laramie, Wyoming 82070
307-745-4020
307-745-8787 (fax)
www.ultracollector.com
info@ultracollector.com
(Note that www.ultracollector.com
appears to be extraordinarily broad-
based and constantly changing.)

Copyright Office
Library of Congress
101 Independence Avenue, S.E.
Washington, D.C. 20559-6000
202-707-3000
www.copyright.gov

International Foundation for Art
Research (IFAR)
(helpful for authenticating works of
art and stolen works)
500 Fifth Avenue, Suite 1234
New York, NY 10110
212-391-6234
212-391-8794 (fax)
www.ifar.org
kferg@ifar.org

Metropolitan Museum of Art
1000 Fifth Avenue
New York, NY 10028-0198
212-535-7710
TTY: 212-650-2921
www.metmuseum.org

Museum of Modern Art
11 West 53rd Street
New York, NY 10019
212-708-9400
www.moma.org

The National Antique and Art Dealers Association of America, Inc.
220 East 57th Street
New York, NY 10022
212-826-9707
212-832-9493 (fax)
www.naadaa.org
inquiries@naadaa.org

Palmer/Wirfs & Associates
(antiques, art and collectibles show promoter)
4001 NE Halsey
Portland, Oregon 97232
503-282-0877
503-282-2953 (fax)
www.palmerwirfs.com

Sotheby's
(international auction house)
1334 York Avenue
New York, NY 10021
212-606-7000
212-606-7107 (fax)
www.sothebys.com

United States Postal Service
(stamp collecting)
www.usps.com/news/2002/philatelic/

See also:
www.philatelic.com
(website only for stamp collecting)

List of Publications

The publications set forth below cover some aspects of collecting and include publications concerning art, antiquities, and the like. Since publications come and go with regularity, it is important for you to verify that the publication is still available. In addition, you can find new magazines and periodicals by checking the periodical index available in most public libraries.

NOTE: *Since the Web is in constant flux and publications are appearing and going out of print with some regularity, no list such as this can be complete, accurate and up to date. The reader is, therefore, urged to independently verify all addresses, phone numbers and, where possible, indices for more current information.*

American Craft
American Craft Council,
Membership Dept.
72 Spring Street
New York, NY 10012
212-274-0630

The Art Business Encyclopedia
By Leonard D. DuBoff (1994)
Allworth Press
10 East 23rd Street
New York, NY 10010
www.allworth.com

Art & Antiques
P.O. Box 11697
Des Moines, IA 50340
800-274-7594

Art in America
P.O. Box 11292
Des Moines, IA 50347-1292
800-925-8059

Art Law in a Nutshell, 3d ed.
by Leonard D. DuBoff
West Publishing Co., 2001
P.O. Box 64526
St. Paul, MN 55164-0526
www.westgroup.com

ARTnews
Subscription Service
P.O. Box 56591
Boulder, CO 80323-6591
800-284-4625

Business Forms & Contracts (In Plain English)® for Craftspeople, 2d ed.
by Leonard D. DuBoff (1993)
Interweave Press
201 E. Fourth Street
Loveland, CO 80537
303-669-7672; 800-272-2193

The Crafts Business Encyclopedia
By Leonard D. DuBoff (1993)
Harcourt, Inc
6277 Sea Harbor Drive
Orlando, FL 32887
407-345-3967

The Deskbook of Art Law, 3d ed.
by Leonard D. DuBoff & Christy O. King (2002)
Oceana Press
75 Main Street
Dobbs Ferry, NY 10522
(914) 693-8100

"Guidelines on Choosing a Conservator"
America Institute for Conservation
1400 16th St., N.W., Suite 340
Washington, DC 20036
(202) 232-6636

The Law (In Plain English)® for Art and Craft Galleries
by Leonard D. DuBoff (1994)
Interweave Press
201 E. Fourth Street
Loveland, CO 80537
303-669-7672; 800-272-2193

The Law (In Plain English)® for Crafts, 5 ed.
by Leonard D. DuBoff (1999)
Allworth Press
10 East 23rd Street
New York, NY 10010
www.allworth.com

The Law (In Plain English)® for Galleries, 2d ed.
By Leonard D. DuBoff
Allworth Press
10 East 23rd Street
New York, NY   10010
www.allworth.com

The Law (In Plain English)® for Photographers, 2d ed.
by Leonard D. DuBoff (2001)
Allworth Press
10 East 23rd Street
New York, NY   10010
www.allworth.com

The Law (In Plain English)® for Small Businesses, 3d ed.
by Leonard D. DuBoff (1998)
Allworth Press
10 East 23rd Street
New York, NY   10010
www.allworth.com

Metalsmith
Society of North American
Goldsmiths (SNAG)
5009 Londonderry Drive
Tampa, FL   33647-9910
813-977-5324

National Calendar of Indoor-Outdoor Art Fairs
by Henry Niles
5423 New Haven Avenue
Fort Wayne, IN   46803

The Photographer's Business and Legal Handbook
by Leonard D. DuBoff
Images Press, Inc., 1989
22 E. 17th Street
New York, NY   10003
212-675-3707

Sculpture
International Sculpture Conference
P.O. Box 91110
Washington, DC   20077-7320
800-221-3148

To obtain other books on crafts art,
antiquities and other collectibles, it
is recommended that you try book
vendors on the Internet, such as:

Amazon.com:
www.amazon.com

Barnes & Noble.com:
www.bn.com

Collectibles Today:
www.collectibles.com

eBay:
www.ebay.com

Schiffer Books
Schifferbooks.com
(Book publisher with more than
2,600 titles relating to antiques, collectibles, art and design, military and
aviation history, craft, and others.)

Selected Laws Governing Artists and Dealers

Laws governing the relationship between artists and dealers have been enacted in twenty-eight states. These laws vary from jurisdiction to jurisdiction and should be consulted to determine whether a transaction is covered.

In this appendix, the laws, by state, are first identified. Following the list are separate sections providing the various states' definitions of art sellers, the types of work covered by each state's statute, and special provisions unique to various states. It is important for you to consult the statute actually in existence when your transaction takes place to verify that the law presented in this appendix has not been amended or repealed. Attorneys who specialize in this area should be consulted when dealing with a transaction covered by this type of legislation.

Alaska	Alaska Stat. Sections 45.65.200 to 45.65.250 (Michie 2002).
Arizona	Ariz. Rev. Stat. Ann. Sections 44-1771 to 1773 (West 2003).
Arkansas	Ark. Stat. Code. Sections 4-73-201 to 207 (Michie 2003).
California	Cal. Civ. Code Section 1738 (Derring 2003).

Colorado	Colo. Rev. Stat. Sections 6-15-101 to 104 (2002).
Connecticut	Conn. Gen. Stat. Ann. Sections 42-116k to 116m (West 2003).
Florida	Fla. Stat. ch. 686.501 to 503 (2002).
Idaho	Idaho Code Sections 28-11-101 to 106 (Michie 2002).
Illinois	815 Ill. Comp. State 320/.01-8 (2003).
Iowa	Iowa Code Sections 556D.1 to 556D.5 (2003).
Kentucky	Ky. Rev. Stat. Ann. Sections 365.850 to 875 (Michie 2002).
Maryland	Md. Com. Law Code Ann. Sections 11-8a-01 to 04 (Michie 2003).
Massachusetts	Mass. Ann. Laws ch. 104a, Sections 1 to 6 (Law. Co-op. 2002).
Michigan	Mich. Comp. Laws Sections 442.311 to 312a (2002).
Minnesota	Minn. Stat. Sections 324.01 to .05 (2002).
Missouri	Mo. Rev. Stat. Sections 407.900 to .910 (2003).

Montana	Mont. Code Ann. Sections 22-2-501 to 505 (2002).
New Hampshire	N.H. Rev. Stat. Ann. Sections 352:3 to 352:12 (2002).
New Jersey	N.J. Rev. Stat. Section 12A:2-330 (2002).
New Mexico	N.M. Stat. Ann. Sections 56-11-1 to 3 (2002).
New York	N.Y. Arts & Cult. Aff. Law Sections 11.01, 12.01 (McKinney 2003).
North Carolina	N.C. Gen. Stat. Sections 25C-1 to 5 (2003).
Ohio	Ohio Rev. Code Ann. Sections 1339.71 to 1339.78 (Anderson 2002).
Oregon	Or. Rev. Stat. Sections 359.200 to 359.255 (2001).
Pennsylvania	73 Pa. Cons. Stat. Sections 2122 to 2130 (2002).
Tennessee	Tenn. Code Ann. Sections 47-25-1001 to 1007 (2002).
Washington	Wash. Rev. Code Ann. Section 18.110 (2003).
Wisconsin	Wis. Stat. Ann. Sections 129.01 to 129.08 (West 2002).

Art Sellers Covered by the Statutes:

Alaska:
"Art dealer" means a person engaged in the business of selling works of art, other than a person exclusively engaged in the business of selling goods at public auction.

Arizona:
"Art dealer" means a person engaged in the business of selling works of fine art, other than a person exclusively engaged in the business of selling goods at public auction.

Arkansas:
"Art dealer" means a person engaged in the business of selling works of art.

California:
"Art dealer" means a person engaged in the business of selling works of fine art, other than a person exclusively engaged in the business of selling goods at public auction.

Colorado:
"Art dealer" means a person engaged in the business of selling works of fine art, other than a person exclusively engaged in the business of selling goods at public auction.

Connecticut:
"Art dealer" means a person, partnership, firm, association or corporation other than a public auctioneer who undertakes to sell works of fine art.

Florida:

"Art dealer" means a person engaged in the business of selling works of art, a person who is a consignee of a work of art, or a person who, by occupation, holds himself out as having knowledge or skill peculiar to works of art or rare documents or prints, or to whom such knowledge or skill may be attributed by his employment of an agent or broker or other intermediary who, by occupation, holds himself out as having such knowledge or skill. The term "art dealer" includes an auctioneer who sells works of art, rare maps, rare documents, or rare prints at public auction as well as the auctioneer's consignor or principal. The term "art dealer" does not include a cooperative which is totally owned by artist members.

Idaho:

"Art dealer" means a person engaged in the business of selling works of fine art, other than a person exclusively engaged in the business of selling goods at public auction.

Illinois:

"Art dealer" means a person engaged in the business of selling works of fine art, other than a person exclusively engaged in the business of selling goods at public auction.

Iowa:

"Art dealer" means a person engaged in the business of selling works of fine art, in a shop or gallery devoted in the majority to works of fine art, other than a person engaged in the business of selling goods of general merchandise or at a public auction.

Kentucky:

"Art dealer" means a person engaged in the business of selling, as either a primary or supplemental source of income, works of fine art, other than a person exclusively engaged in the business of selling goods at public auction.

Maryland:

"Art dealer" means an individual, partnership, firm, association, or corporation, other than a public auctioneer, that undertakes to sell a work of fine art created by someone else.

Massachusetts:

"Art dealer" means a person engaged in the business of selling works of fine art, other than a person exclusively engaged in the business of selling goods at public auction.

Michigan:

"Art dealer" means a person engaged in the business of selling works of fine art, other than a person exclusively engaged in the business of selling goods at public auction.

Minnesota:

"Art dealer" means a person engaged in the business of selling works of fine art, other than a person exclusively engaged in the business of selling goods at public auction.

Missouri:

The term "art dealer" means a person engaged in the business of selling fine arts. The term "art dealer" does not include any person engaged exclusively in the business of selling goods at public auction.

Montana:

"Art dealer" means a person engaged in the business of selling works of fine art, other than a person exclusively engaged in the business of selling goods at public auction.

New Hampshire:

"Art dealer" means a person, including an individual, partnership, firm, association, or corporation, engaged in the business of selling works of art, other than a person exclusively engaged in the business of selling goods at a public auction.

New Jersey:

"Art dealer" means a person engaged in the business of selling crafts and works of fine art, other than a person exclusively engaged in the business of selling goods at public auction.

New Mexico:

"Art dealer" means a person primarily engaged in the business of selling works of art.

New York:

"Art merchant" means a person who is in the business of dealing, exclusively or non-exclusively, in works of fine art or multiples, or a person who by his occupation holds himself out as having knowledge or skill peculiar to such works, or to whom such knowledge or skill may be attributed by his employment of an agent or other intermediary who by his occupation holds himself out as having such knowledge or skill. The term "art merchant" includes an auctioneer who sells such works at public auction, and except in the case of multiples, includes persons, not otherwise defined or treated as art merchants herein, who are consignors or principals of auctioneers.

North Carolina:
"Art dealer" means an individual, partnership, firm, association, or corporation that undertakes to sell a work of fine art created by someone else.

Ohio:
"Art dealer" means a person engaged in the business of selling works of art, other than a person exclusively engaged in the business of selling goods at public auction.

Oregon:
"Art dealer" means a person, other than a public auctioneer, who undertakes to sell a work of fine art created by another.

Pennsylvania:
"Art dealer." A person engaged in the business of selling crafts and works of fine art, other than a person exclusively engaged in the business of selling goods at public auction.

Tennessee:
"Art dealer" means a person engaged in the business of selling works of art, other than a person exclusively engaged in the business of selling goods at public auction.

Washington:
"Art dealer" means a person, partnership, firm, association or corporation, other than a public auctioneer, which undertakes to sell a work of fine art created by another.

Wisconsin:
"Art dealer" means a person engaged in the business of selling works of fine art, other than a person exclusively engaged in the business of selling goods at public auction.

Art Works **Protected by State Statutes:**

Alaska:
"Work of art" means an original or multiple original art work including: (A) visual art such as a painting, sculpture, drawing, mosaic, or photograph; (B) calligraphy; (C) graphic art such as an etching, lithograph, offset print, or silk screen; (D) craft work in clay, textile, fiber, wood, metal, plastic, or glass materials; (E) mixed media such as a collage or any combination of art media in this paragraph; (F) art employing traditional native materials such as ivory, bone, grass, baleen, animal skins, wood and furs.

Arizona:
"Work of fine art" means an original or multiple original art work which is: (a) A visual rendition, including a painting, drawing, sculpture, mosaic or photograph. (b) A work of calligraphy. (c) A work of graphic art, including an etching, lithograph, offset print or silkscreen. (d) A craft work in materials, including clay, textile, fiber, wood, metal, plastic or glass. (e) A work in mixed media, including a collage or a work consisting of any combination of subdivisions (a) through (d).

Arkansas:
"Art" means a painting, sculpture, drawing, work of graphic art, pottery, weaving, batik, macrame, quilt, or other commonly recognized art form.

California:
"Fine art" means a painting, sculpture, drawing, work of graphic art (including an etching, lithograph, offset print, silk screen, or a work of graphic art of like nature), a work of calligraphy, or a work in mixed media (including a collage, assemblage, or any combination of the foregoing art media).

Colorado:

"Work of fine art" or "work" means: (a) A work of visual art such as a painting, sculpture, drawing, mosaic or photograph; (b) A work of calligraphy; (c) A work of graphic art such as an etching, a lithograph, an offset print, a silk screen, or any other work of similar nature; (d) A craft work in materials, including but not limited to clay, textile, fiber, wood, metal, plastic, or glass; (e) A work in mixed media such as a collage or any combination of the art media set forth in this subsection.

Connecticut:

"Fine art" means (1) a work of visual art such as a painting, sculpture, drawing, mosaic or photograph; (2) a work of calligraphy; (3) a work of graphic art such as an etching, lithograph, offset print, silk screen, or other work of graphic art of like nature; (4) crafts such as crafts in clay, textile, fiber, wood, metal, plastic, glass or similar materials; and (5) a work in mixed media such as a collage or any combination of the foregoing art media.

Florida:

"Art" means a painting, sculpture, drawing, work of graphic art, pottery, weaving, batik, macrame, quilt, print, photograph, or craft work executed in materials including, but not limited to, clay, textile, paper, fiber, wood, tile, metal, plastic, or glass. The term shall also include a rare map which is offered as a limited edition or a map 80 years old or older; or a rare document or rare print which includes, but is not limited to, a print, engraving, etching, woodcut, lithograph, or serigraph which is offered as a limited edition, or one 80 years old or older.

Idaho:

"Fine art" means a painting, sculpture, drawing, work of graphic art, including an etching, lithograph, signed limited edition offset print, silk screen, or a work of graphic art of like nature; a work of calligraphy, photographs, original works in ceramics, wood, metals, glass, plastic, wax, stone or leather or a work in mixed media, including a collage, assemblage, or any combination of the art media mentioned in this subsection.

Illinois:

"Work of fine art" means: (a) A visual rendition including, but not limited to, a painting, drawing, sculpture, mosaic, videotape, or photograph. (b) A work of calligraphy. (c) A work of graphic art including, but not limited to, an etching, lithograph, serigraph, or offset print. (d) A craft work in materials including, but not limited to, clay, textile, fiber, wood, metal, plastic, or glass. (e) A work in mixed media including, but not limited to, a collage, assemblage, or work consisting of any combination of paragraphs (a) through (d).

Iowa:

"Fine art" means a painting, sculpture, drawing, mosaic, photograph, work of graphic art, including an etching, lithograph, offset print, silk screen, or work of graphic art of like nature, a work of calligraphy, or a work in mixed media including a collage, assemblage, or any combination of these art media which is one of a kind or is available in a limited issue or series.

"Fine art" also means crafts that include work in clay, textiles, fiber, wood, metal, plastic, glass, or similar materials which is one of a kind or is available in a limited issue or series.

Kentucky:

"Fine art" shall include, but is not limited to, a painting, sculpture, drawing, work of graphic or photographic art, including an etching, lithograph, offset print, silk screen, or work of graphic art of like nature, a work of calligraphy, a work of folk art or craft, or a work in mixed media including a collage, assemblage, or any combination of the foregoing art media.

Maryland:

"Work of fine art" means an original art work which is: (1) A visual rendition including a painting, drawing, sculpture, mosaic, or photograph; (2) A work of calligraphy; (3) A work of graphic art including an etching, lithograph, offset print, or silk screen; (4) A craft work in materials including clay, textile, fiber, wood, metal, plastic, or glass; or (5) A work in mixed media including a collage or a work consisting of any combination of works included in this subsection.

Massachusetts:

"Fine art," a painting, sculpture, drawing, work of graphic art, including an etching, lithograph, offset print, silk screen, or work of graphic art of like nature, a work of calligraphy, or a work in mixed media including a collage, assemblage, or any combination of the foregoing art media.

Michigan:

"Art" means a painting, sculpture, drawing, work of graphic art, photograph, weaving, or work of craft art.

Minnesota:

"Art" means a painting, sculpture, drawing, work of graphic art, photograph, weaving, or work of craft art.

Missouri:

The term "fine arts" includes: (a) Visual art such as paintings, sculptures, drawings, mosaics, or photographs; (b) Calligraphy; (c) Graphic art such as etchings, lithographs, offset prints, silk screens, and other works of a similar nature; (d) Crafts, including any item made by an artist or craftsman through the use of clay, textiles, fibers, wood, metal, plastic, glass, ceramics, or similar materials; (e) Works in mixed media such as collages or any combination of the art forms or media listed in paragraph (a), (b), (c), or (d) of this subdivision.

Montana:
"Fine art" means a painting, sculpture, drawing, work of graphic art (including an etching, lithograph, signed limited edition offset print, silk screen, or work of graphic art of like nature), a work of calligraphy, photographs, original works in ceramics, wood, metals, glass, plastic, wax, stone, or leather, or a work in mixed media (including a collage, assemblage, or any combination of the art media mentioned in this subsection).

New Hampshire:
"Work of art" means an original art work that is any of the following: (a) A visual rendition including, but not limited to, a painting, drawing, sculpture, mosaic, or photograph. (b) A work of calligraphy. (c) A work of graphic art, including, but not limited to, an etching, lithograph, offset print, silk screen, or other work of similar materials. (d) A craft work in materials, including, but not limited to, clay, textile, fiber, wood, metal, plastic, glass, or similar materials. (e) A work in mixed media, including, but not limited to, a collage or a work consisting of any combination of the items listed in subparagraphs (a) through (d) of this paragraph.

New Jersey:
"Craft" means an artistic rendition created using any medium, including, but not limited to, a collage and other works consisting of any combination of painting, drawing, sculpture, photography and manual creation in clay, textile, fiber, wood, metal, plastic, glass, stone, leather or similar materials.

"Fine art" means an original work of visual or graphic art created using any medium, including but not limited to, a painting, drawing or sculpture.

New Mexico:
"Art" means a painting, sculpture, drawing, work of graphic art, pottery, weaving, batik, macrame or quilt containing the artist's original handwritten signature on the work of art.

New York:
"Craft" means a functional or non-functional work individually designed, and crafted by hand, in any medium including but not limited to textile, tile, paper, clay, glass, fiber, wood, metal or plastic; provided, however, that if produced in multiples, craft shall not include works mass produced or produced in other than a limited edition.
"Fine art" means a painting, sculpture, drawing, or work of graphic art, and print, but not multiples.

North Carolina:
"Work of fine art" means an original art work that is: (a) A visual rendition, including a painting, drawing, sculpture, mosaic, or photograph; (b) A work of calligraphy; (c) A work of graphic art, including an etching, lithograph, offset print, or silk screen; (d) A craft work in materials, including clay, textile, fiber, wood, metal, plastic, or glass; or (e) A work in mixed media, including a collage or a work consisting of any combination of works included in this subdivision.

Ohio:
"Work of art" means an original art work that is any of the following: (1) A visual rendition including, but not limited to, a painting, drawing, sculpture, mosaic, or photograph; (2) A work of calligraphy; (3 |) A work of graphic art, including, but not limited to, an etching, lithograph, offset print, or silk screen; (4) A craft work in materials, including, but not limited to, clay, textile, fiber, wood, metal, plastic, or glass; (5) A work in mixed media, including, but not limited to, a collage or a work consisting of any combination of the items listed in divisions (D)(1) to (4) of this section.

Oregon:
"Fine art" means: (a) An original work of visual art such as a painting, sculpture, drawing, mosaic or photograph; (b) A work in calligraphy; (c) A work of graphic art such as an etching, lithograph, offset print, silk screen or other work of similar nature; (d) A craft work in materials including but not limited to clay, textile, fiber, wood, metal, plastic, glass or similar materials; or (e) A work in mixed media such as a collage or any combination of the art media described in this subsection.

Pennsylvania:
"Craft." An artistic rendition, created using any medium, including, but not limited to, a collage and other works consisting of any combination of painting, drawing, sculpture, photography and manual creation in clay, textile, fiber, wood, metal, plastic, glass, stone, leather or similar materials.

"Fine art." An original work of visual or graphic art of recognized quality, created using any medium, including, but not limited to, a painting, drawing or sculpture.

Tennessee:
"Work of art" means an original art work which is: (A) A visual rendition, including a painting, drawing, sculpture, mosaic, or photograph; (B) A work of calligraphy; (C) A work of graphic art, including an etching, lithograph, offset print, or silk screen; (D) A craft work in materials, including clay, textile, fiber, wood, metal, plastic, or glass; or (E) A work in mixed media, including a collage or a work consisting of any combination of subdivisions (6)(A) through (6)(D).

Washington:
"Work of fine art" means an original art work which is: (a) A visual rendition including a painting, drawing, sculpture, mosaic, or photograph; (b) A work of calligraphy; (c) A work of graphic art including

an etching, lithograph, offset print, or silk screen; (d) A craft work in materials including clay, textile, fiber, wood, metal, plastic, or glass; or (e) A work in mixed media including a collage or a work consisting of any combination of works included in this subsection.

Wisconsin:

"Work of fine art" means an original art work which is: (a) A visual rendition including, but not limited to, a painting, drawing, sculpture, mosaic, or photograph; (b) A work of calligraphy; (c) A work of graphic art, including, but not limited to, an etching, lithograph, offset print or silk screen; (d) A craft work in materials, including but not limited to clay, textile, fiber, wood, metal, plastic or glass; (e) A work in mixed media, including, but not limited to, a collage or a work consisting of any combination of pars. (a) to (d).

Special Provisions:

Alaska:

Artist-consignor may waive the right to trust-property protection, if such waiver is clear, conspicuous, and agreed to in writing by the artist. No waiver is valid with respect to proceeds from work initially placed on consignment but later purchased by the art dealer-consignee. Nor shall any waiver inure to the benefit of the consignee's creditors in a manner inconsistent with the artist's rights.

Arizona:

Any waiver by artist is void. An art dealer who violates the statute is liable to the artist for damages of $50 plus actual damages, including incidental and consequential damages, sustained by the artist, and reasonable attorney fees.

Arkansas:
Any waiver by artist is void. An art dealer who violates the statute is liable to the artist for a civil penalty of $50 plus actual damages, including incidental and consequential damages, sustained by the artist. Reasonable attorneys' fees and court cost shall be paid the prevailing party.

California:
Any waiver by artist is void.

Colorado:
Any waiver by artist is void. An art dealer who violates the statute is liable to the artist for a civil penalty of $50 plus actual damages, including incidental and consequential damages, sustained by the artist. Reasonable attorneys' fees and court cost shall be paid the prevailing party.

Connecticut:
Any waiver by artist is void. Artist-consignor is required to give notice to the public by placing a tag on the work stating that it is being sold under consignment or by posting a conspicuous sign in consignee's place of business giving notice that some works are being sold under consignment. Statute requires a written agreement covering (1) payment schedule for sale proceeds; (2) responsibility of gallery for loss or damage; (3) written agreement as to retail prices; and (4) artist's written consent to displays and credit on displays.

Florida:
Any waiver by artist is void. Artist-consignor is required to give notice to the public by placing a tag on the work stating that it is being sold under consignment or by posting a conspicuous sign in consignee's place of business giving notice that some works are being sold under consignment.

Idaho:
The art dealer, after delivery of the work of fine art, is an agent of the artist for the purpose of sale or exhibition of the consigned work of fine art within the state of Idaho. This relationship shall be defined in writing and renewed at least every three (3) years by the art dealer and the artist. It is the responsibility of the artist to identify clearly the work of art by securely attaching identifying marking to or clearly signing the work of art.

Illinois:
If the sale of the work of fine art is on installment, the funds from the installment shall first be applied to pay any balance due to the artist on the sale, unless the parties expressly agree in writing that the proceeds on each installment shall be paid according to a percentage established by the consignment agreement. Customer deposits shall be used to pay the amounts due the artist within 30 days after such deposits become part of the payment for the work. Any agreement entered into pursuant to this subsection must be clear and conspicuous.

Iowa:
Any waiver by artist is void.

Kentucky:
None.

Maryland:
None

Massachusetts:
Artist can give written waiver of right to have sale proceeds applied first to pay any balance due artist. If gallery buys artworks for its own account, proceeds shall be trust funds until artist is paid in full.

Michigan:
Artist may waive right to have sale proceeds in any twelve month period in excess of $2500 considered trust funds. If gallery buys the artwork, artist must be paid in full and no waiver of trust fund provision is permitted.

Minnesota:
None.

Missouri:
None.

Montana:
None.

New Hampshire:
None.

New Jersey:
None.

New Mexico:
None.

New York:
Artist-consignor may waive the right to trust-property protection of sale proceeds exceeding $2500 in any twelve month period beginning with the date of the waiver. To be valid, such waiver must be clear, conspicuous, in writing, and signed by the consignor. No waiver is valid with respect to proceeds from work initially placed on consignment but later purchased by the art dealer-consignee. Nor shall any waiver inure to the benefit of the consignee's creditors in a manner inconsistent with the artist's rights.

North Carolina:
None.

Ohio:
None.

Oregon:
The art dealer may accept a work of fine art on consignment only if the dealer and artist enter into a written contract establishing: (1) the retail value of the work; (2) the time within which the proceeds of the sale are to be paid to the artist; (3) the minimum price for the sale of the work; (4) the percentage of the proceeds to be retained by the dealer. Any provision of a contract or agreement whereby the consignor waives any of the statute is void.

Pennsylvania:
None.

Tennessee:
None.

Washington:
The art dealer may accept a work of fine art on consignment only if the art dealer enters into a written contract with the artist which states: (a) the value of the work; (b) the minimum price for the sale of the work; (c) the fee, commission, or other compensation basis of the art dealer. Any portion of a contract that waives any portion of this statute is void. The gallery can only display the work if notice is given that it is the work of the artist and artist gives prior written consent to the particular use or display. If the gallery violates the statute, it is liable to the artist for $50 plus actual damages, and the artist's obligation for compensation to the dealer is voidable. The court may award the artist reasonable attorney's fees.

Wisconsin:

Statute requires a written contract that establishes: (1) an agreed on value for the artwork; (2) the time after sale in which payments must be made to the artist; and (3) the minimum sale price for the consigned artworks. If the gallery fails to enter into such a written contract, a court can void the artist's obligations to the gallery. Also, the gallery can only display an artwork if it credits the artist as creator and has the artist's consent to the particular display. If the gallery violates the statute it must pay the artist $50 plus actual damages and attorney's fees.

Other Resources

The organizations listed below are each involved in some aspect of the world of art, antiquities, and other collectibles. This is by no means a complete and comprehensive list. Consult your local Yellow Pages and/or ask a local museum professional for recommendations. The purpose of this appendix is to provide a cross-section of organizations that deal with some aspect of collecting art, antiquities, and virtually all other forms of collectibles. Here, too, the World Wide Web is an extremely useful tool.

NOTE: *Since the Web is in constant flux and websites are appearing and disappearing with some regularity, no list such as this can be complete, accurate and up to date. The reader is, there-fore, urged to independently verify all addresses, phone numbers and, where possible, indices for more current information.*

CONSERVATION

Western Association of Art Conservation
http://palimpsest.stanford.edu/waac/

INSURANCE

Collectibles Insurance Agency
P.O. Box 1200
Westminster, MD 21158
888-837-9537
Fax: 410-876-9233
International: 410-876-8833
Email: info@insurecollectibles.com
www.collectinsure.com

MUSEUMS
http://icom.museum/museum_directories.html

THEFT-RELATED RESOURCES

The Art Loss Register
20 East 46th Street, Suite 1402
New York, NY 10017
212-297 0941
Fax: 212-972 5091
www.artloss.com

The Art Newspaper
http://www.theartnewspaper.com/looted/lootedart.asp

Art Loss Register
http://www.saztv.com/page9.html

International Foundation for Art Research (IFAR)
500 Fifth Avenue, Suite 1234
New York, NY 10110
212-391-6234
Fax: 212-391-8794
www.ifar.org

Federal Bureau of Investigation (FBI)
U.S. Department of Justice
www.fbi.gov

Interpol
www.interpol.com / www.interpol.int

Links: to sites with links to various registers relating to stolen works
www.museumstuff.com/links/art/stolen/
www.lapada.co.uk/gateway/theft.html

Index

Dedication

To my mother Millicent for teaching me to love beautiful things;
to my wife Mary Ann for sharing that love with me; and to my
grandson Brian, who will hopefully carry on our tradition.

About the Author

Leonard D. DuBoff is an art lover and enthusiast with over thirty years experience studying, teaching, writing, and breathing art and crafts law. Known as one of the leading authorities on Art Law, DuBoff's works are frequently referenced by judges, lawyers, and anyone interested in knowing about the law in this field. He has served on numerous advisory boards and received several accolades for his work and devotion including the Oregon Governor's Art Award.

DuBoff began his renowned career teaching law at Stanford Law School. He then taught as a Professor of Law at Lewis & Clark College in Portland, Oregon, for over twenty-three years. In addition to teaching such courses as the Law and the Arts, DuBoff served Of Counsel to three Portland area law firms before founding The DuBoff Law Group.

DuBoff is licensed to practice in both New York and Oregon, as well as admitted to over fifteen federal courts—including the United States Customs Court, the United States Court of International Trade, and the United States Supreme Court. His major practice areas include Art Law, Crafts law, International Law, Copyright and Trademark Law, and Business Law.

DuBoff's influence is immense. He is the author of over fifteen books directly related to art, crafts, galleries, photographers, and publishing, as well as countless articles on the subject. In addition to *The Antique and Art Collector's Legal Guide*, DuBoff can be found as a frequent contributor to *Art Trends Magazine*, *Communication Arts*, *Glass Craftsman*, *Picture Magazine*, *Woodshop News*, and *Critical Issues*.

DuBoff shares his passion with his wife and three children. He currently lives in Portland, Oregon.